Gitlow v. New York

LANDMARK LAW CASES

AMERICAN SOCIETY

Peter Charles Hoffer

N. E. H. Hull

Series Editors

For a complete list of titles in the series go to www.kansaspress.ku.edu.

MARC LENDLER

Gitlow v. New York

Every Idea an Incitement

UNIVERSITY PRESS OF KANSAS

Published by the University Press of Kansas (Lawrence, Kansas 66045), which was organized by the Kansas Board of Regents and is operated and funded by Emporia State University, Fort Hays State University, Kansas State University, Pittsburg State University, the University of Kansas, and Wichita State University

Library of Congress Cataloging-in-Publication Data

Lendler, Marc (Marc R.)

Gitlow v. New York : every idea an incitement / Marc Lendler.

p. cm. — (Landmark law cases and American society)

Includes bibliographical references and index.

ISBN 978-0-7006-1875-0 (cloth : alk. paper)

ISBN 978-0-7006-1876-7 (pbk. : alk. paper)

1. Gitlow, Benjamin, 1891–1965 — Trials, litigation, etc. 2. Freedom of speech — United States. 3. Freedom of the press — United States. 4. Due process of law — United States. 5. United States. Constitution. 1st Amendment. 6. United States. Constitution. 14th Amendment. 7. Communist trials — United States. 8. Radicalism — United States. 9. Trials (Conspiracy) — United States. I. Title.

KF228.G58L46 2012

345.73'0231 — DC23

2012016669

British Library Cataloguing-in-Publication Data is available.

Printed in the United States of America

10 9 8 7 6 5 4 3 2 1

The paper used in this publication is recycled and contains 30 percent postconsumer waste. It is acid free and meets the minimum requirements of the American National Standard for Permanence of Paper for Printed Library Materials z39.48-1992.

John Stuart Mill wrote that the real victims of

speech censorship are future generations.

This book is dedicated to my own favorite future generation:

Sophia, Velia, Theo, and Dylan.

CONTENTS

EDITORS' PREFACE

From colonial times, the "bad or evil tendency" test for seditious speech and press has permeated American law, chilling free expression and providing almost untrammeled discretion for state and federal prosecutors to silence their critics. The doctrine is simple: criticism of the government that tends to undermine public confidence is a crime; speech or writing that might cause disobedience to law is a crime. The First Amendment to the federal Constitution and parallel provisions in state constitutions notwithstanding, federal and state law has punished seditious speech because of its tendency — no act in furtherance of the perceived threat to public order was necessary. The speech or writing itself was sufficient to trigger the penalty.

Marc Lendler tracks one of the most (in)famous cases of this kind: the conviction of Communist organizer Benjamin Gitlow for writing and publishing a left-wing manifesto. Gitlow was tried and convicted under a New York State criminal anarchy statute penalizing "the advocacy by word of mouth or writing . . . the doctrine that organized government should be overthrown by force or violence, or by assassination of the executive head or of any of the executive officials of government, or by any unlawful means," in the wake of New York's version of the Red Scare raids after World War I. Gitlow appealed his case to the New York Court of Appeals and then to the federal courts. Here, Lendler finds Gitlow guilty of violating the letter of the law: he wanted the violent overthrow of the government, and his crime was producing a pamphlet advocating that event. But little did his detractors or his defenders anticipate that this case would become the vehicle for the Supreme Court's incorporation of the First Amendment — that is, its imposition on the states — and for a ringing dissent that remains one of the finest defenses of the principle of free speech.

Gitlow v. New York (1925) is a case taught in every constitutional law course, but Lendler offers something far beyond the accounts in casebooks and hornbooks. He brings the case alive. We meet Gitlow, a dogged and unrepentant radical, as well as his parents and his friends. They were activists and idealists who, if misguided in retrospect, were sincere in their beliefs. War and repression further radicalized him, turning a Socialist assemblyman into a believer in the Bolshevik revolution and an advocate of the Soviet Union. With the United States in an undeclared war with the Bolshevik regime, postwar labor agitation growing, and anti-Soviet hysteria mounting, Gitlow became an easy target for prosecution under the New York law. Former New York City police commissioner William McAdoo would be the Javier to Gitlow's Jean Valjean, pressing the prosecution, upping the stakes, and all but dictating the outcome. The trial judge, Bartow Weeks, was no more sympathetic, ordering Gitlow to serve his full term of imprisonment at hard labor. With Gitlow's fate apparently sealed, New York tried and convicted his fellow Communists. In vain, their counsel argued that the New York law revived some of the worst aspects of the hated Sedition Act of 1798.

But Gitlow's fate was not sealed. Though he surely would have been pardoned by Governor Al Smith (his codefendants were), he preferred to appeal his case as high as it could go. As his story unfolds here, we meet some of the most important figures in early-twentieth-century American law: famous criminal defense attorney Clarence Darrow, who represented Gitlow at his trial and told the jury, "for a man to be afraid of revolution in America" is to ignore our own history; New York Court of Appeals justices Cuthbert Pound and Benjamin Cardozo, whose dissent argued that Gitlow's manifesto was "a negligible philosophical abstraction" when unaccompanied by any action; Walter Pollak of the American Civil Liberties Union, who carried the appeal to the U.S. Supreme Court, insisting, "our contention is that the statute . . . is unconstitutional"; and Supreme Court justices Oliver Wendell Holmes Jr. and Louis Brandeis, whose dissent concluded that "the only meaning of free speech is that [ideas] should be given their chance" to be heard. After all, there was "no present danger" in Gitlow's words.

The quality of Lendler's research, the wise balance in his treatment of both sides of the case, and the clarity of his explanation of the developing notions of free speech enhance his handling of the human story. And the last of these — Gitlow's return to Sing Sing and his eventual pardon, his continuing advocacy of international Communism, and, in his later days, his work as an anti-Communist activist —

provides a fitting climax to the book. Lendler has assembled all the facts. He has traced the twists and turns of free speech jurisprudence and the incorporation doctrine through the end of the Cold War. In the end, he offers his own judgment, but whatever one's own verdict, this account is essential reading.

ACKNOWLEDGMENTS

In the nine years between this book's conception and completion, a number of people have provided help and direction that were indispensable. My first task after deciding that the *Gitlow* case was worth exploring was to see whether a transcript of the trial still existed. Fortunately, I was directed to David Badertscher, librarian at the New York Supreme Court Law Library, who was both knowledgeable and very helpful; he located the *Gitlow* transcript, and those of the four related trials discussed in chapters 2 and 4, and let me sit in the library's microfilm room for eight hours a day over several months.

My next task was to learn more about Ben Gitlow himself. I benefited greatly at the outset from an extended interview with Ben Gitlow Jr. and several subsequent communications with him. The archivists at the Special Collections section of the Murray Atkins Library at the University of North Carolina at Charlotte and at the Hoover Institute, the two places where Gitlow's papers are held, made it easy to find, access, and copy relevant material during my many trips to both. It would have been difficult to interpret the early American Communist world without the help of Tim Davenport, whose knowledge of matters large and small — from factions to aliases — was of invaluable assistance. Other private communications are listed in the bibliographic essay, but I want to mention two that offered unique insight: Lawrence Fruchter, son of Gitlow's sister Bella, and Judy Branfman, niece of Yetta Stromberg.

I also needed to look at cases for which *Gitlow* was a precedent. Sika Berger, social science librarian at Smith College, was instrumental in pointing out ways to do that. Nicole Martinez and Boe Morgan, students at the time, worked as research assistants in collecting some of that information. Jessica Cepriano and Erin Dow, two former students who are now lawyers in New York, helped explain some particulars of New York law.

Others who provided important help once I reached the writing phase include Maeva Marcus, who pointed me toward the University Press of Kansas; David Rabban, who commented on a shorter form of my *Gitlow* argument in a panel discussion; readers Paul Kens, Daniel Leab, and Geoffrey Stone; series editor Paul Hoffer; and the press's editor in chief, Michael Briggs. I should also mention that it was Paul Kens's *Judicial Power and Reform Politics* about the *Lochner* case, as well as Richard Polenberg's *Fighting Faiths* about the *Abrams* case, that convinced me of the value of an in-depth examination of a single Supreme Court decision and of including biographical information about the principals.

It was my wife, Dianne, who mastered the most useful skill in the many years I spent with this topic: fleeing the room whenever friends asked the obvious question: "Oh, what are you writing a book about?" At least now the answer will be tangible.

Gitlow v. New York

Introduction

In 1901 President William McKinley was shot and killed in Buffalo, New York. His deranged assassin, Leon Czolgosz, had a passing acquaintance with anarchism and had attended a lecture by America's most famous anarchist, Emma Goldman. Czolgosz was tried and executed, but authorities in New York expressed regrets that there was no law available to charge Goldman, who, they believed, had "caused" the crime with her speeches and writings and further infuriated them by writing sympathetically about Czolgosz. The lack of any legal avenue to pursue Goldman led the New York legislature to pass a criminal anarchy law in 1902, making it a felony to advocate "the doctrine that organized government should be overthrown by force or violence . . . or by any illegal means." The law lay there, unused, until the set of events that eventually led the Supreme Court to consider the case of *Gitlow v. New York* in 1925.

Ben Gitlow was one of the founders of the American Communist Party, and his 1919 arrest and trial were part of a New York version of the better-known Palmer raids, which followed two months later. If his name rings any bells today, it is probably because undergraduates and law students recognize his case as the one that began the "incorporation" of the Bill of Rights — the gradual process by which rights were guaranteed against state as well as federal infringement.

The extension of the Bill of Rights is the most important legacy of *Gitlow*. But it is significant on several other grounds as well; many paths led to and from this case. The prosecutors and judges who sustained Gitlow's conviction provided some of the clearest and most instructive examples of the "bad tendency" doctrine — that speakers are responsible for the reasonable, probable outcome of their words, irrespective of how likely it is that those words will create an overt criminal act. Gitlow, inspired by the Russian Revolution, envisioned

{ 1 }

a Soviet America, and his writings and speeches were intended to bring that about. To the state of New York, that was enough to create a crime; whether his words were likely to persuade anyone to do anything illegal was beside the point. The Supreme Court would eventually agree, explicitly endorsing the bad tendency principle. The Court added another, more original reason to uphold the conviction – that the New York legislature had the right to name doctrines that were harmful at any time, and the courts had no role to play in looking at potential effects or circumstances.

The dissent in the Supreme Court was also of lasting significance. Oliver Wendell Holmes, joined by Louis Brandeis, took issue with the bad tendency doctrine in one of a series of dissents that eventually redefined the Court's reasoning about speech rights. His dissent in this case was short but controversial, and it still has critics, despite the fact that the views he and Brandeis advocated have become mainstream Court doctrine.

The first half of the book outlines why the "Left Wing Manifesto" – the treatise that led to Gitlow's arrest – was written, what its purposes were, and how the prosecution argued for conviction almost exclusively on the basis of that writing. The purpose is to demonstrate what the passage of time sometimes obscures, which, in this case, is that the prosecution's argument was accurate: Gitlow intended to bring about change by illegal means. Gitlow himself admitted as much, both at the time and even more strongly in later years, when he became a vehement anti-Communist. He and the others tried on the same charges (see chapter 4) were transfixed by the Soviet revolution, tried to import its Bolshevik principles to the United States, made frequent trips to Moscow, and sometimes brought back funds to aid the American Communist Party. Those facts were not the products of prosecutorial invention or the imagination of overzealous anti-Communists. The validity of the bad tendency doctrine is best weighed when the tendency really is "bad" – that is, when the state does not exaggerate the harm a defendant's views might cause. In *Gitlow v. New York*, it did not.

The second half of the book follows the case up the judicial ladder after Gitlow's conviction. He agreed to let the fledgling American Civil Liberties Union appeal his case to test the constitutionality of a law that prohibits a specific doctrine. The appeals found no support in New York courts. The case eventually arrived at a Supreme Court that had been divided for some time over the scope of the Fourteenth Amendment and more recently over the First Amendment. Chapter 6 outlines how these divergent lines came together to lead to the incorporation doctrine and examines the disagreement between the *Gitlow* majority and Holmes over the substance of First Amendment protection. As the Court's thinking on speech rights evolved in the direction pioneered by Holmes and Brandeis, it had to deal with the *Gitlow* precedent often in the next forty years. In particular, because the Communist cases of the early Cold War era shared so many features with *Gitlow*, the Court had to revisit it, walking a very fine line to avoid repudiating Holmes directly while upholding the convictions of Communist leaders. The ebb and flow of *Gitlow* as a precedent are the subject of chapter 7.

In the mid-1980s Benjamin Gitlow Jr. was in a jury pool for a tax case. The judge asked, among other routine questions, whether any of the potential jurors had any family members who had been convicted of a felony. Ben Jr. raised his hand. The judge looked down the list of jurors' names, and when the significance of Ben's name dawned on him, he said, "Come up here. Are you [the son of] *that* one?" He dismissed Ben Jr. from the jury pool, then joined the two lawyers in sending him off with handshakes and stories about studying *Gitlow vs. New York*. Both son and father knew that the latter's Supreme Court case was famous, but neither understood exactly why. The rest of this book explains that, although the underlying reason can be stated simply: Every era revisits the bad tendency principle in light of whatever relationship between words and harmful acts seems especially threatening at the time. In 1919 the problem was the possibility of class conflict and revolution. At the start of the Cold War the fear was that activity by domestic supporters of the Soviet Union might be harmful to national security. In the contemporary era the debates have involved graphic descriptions of violence in books, in movies, or on the Internet; speech denigrating ethnic groups or women; and speech supporting Islamic radicalism. In the future the subject will be different, but the debate will be the same: how should the law be applied to words that might lead to crimes? In those debates, a look back at *Gitlow*'s arguments and its standing as a precedent will be unavoidable.

CHAPTER I

Famous Long Ago

Bear with me, then, as I present a few episodes of the exciting
drama of our time, for history is the passion and restless spirit that
is man in which the last act is yet to be played.

BEN GITLOW, UNPUBLISHED MANUSCRIPT

For someone whose life was full of dramatic confrontation and ideological switchbacks, Benjamin Gitlow's early entry into Socialist politics seemed almost preordained, more osmosis than decision. His
Russian Jewish immigrant parents, Louis and Kate Golman Gitlow,
had been freethinkers and opponents of the czar. Ben noted in a mem-
oir that Louis and Kate "broke with the religious traditions of their
parents, their marriage being conceived in freedom and without rab-
bis or civil authorities giving their seal of approval." The Gitlows emi-
grated from Russia in part so that Louis could avoid serving in the
czarist military. Louis left Russia first; Kate left the next year after giving birth to their first child. Ben was born in Elizabethport, New Jersey, in 1891, and a later letter from his mother described his birth as a
kind of Socialist omen: "You were born into the world a very big baby
with a big kick, as though protesting. . . . So you were born with a
protest against conditions and continued to protest and fight for a better system."

A year later the Gitlows moved to a tenement on Cherry Street,
part of the Jewish, eastern European immigrant community on the
Lower East Side of Manhattan. Louis, who had studied to be a civil
engineer in Russia, operated a sewing machine in a garment factory;
Kate finished shirts at home. In a letter to Ben, Kate Gitlow described
her husband carrying his sewing machine on his back from place to
place and confided that she had told Louis she would break the
machine if he did not stop working past midnight at home.

Ben's most vivid memories were not those of hardship but of the anticzarist ferment among recent émigrés, of "the sociability prevailing in my parents' home . . . the Socialist activities that emanated from our home, the discussion and stories that the immigrants told about their personal and political experiences in Czarist Russia." Louis and Kate were both ardent Socialists. Louis edited a left-wing newspaper called the *Voice of Labor*, and both were active members of the Socialist Labor Party. They entertained a constant flow of immigrant leftists of all kinds, and Ben described growing up in this environment in his autobiography, *I Confess:* "I thrilled at the stories of the underground movement, of the conspiring activities, how deeds of violence against the Tsarist oppressors were planned. . . . I heard the stories about the Molly McGuires, the Homestead Steel Strike, the heroism of the anarchist martyrs. . . . I listened to discussions, very idealistic in their essence, in which the participants showed how Socialism would transform the world." He recalled his mother staying up at night, reading and translating Russian and Yiddish poets for the children. Kate would later join the Communist Labor Party with her son, and she teamed with Clara Lemlich, leader of the 1909 strike in the garment industry, to form the United Council of Working Class Housewives. Kate became a prominent party figure in the 1920s, only to be expelled with Ben in 1929.

In his published autobiography, Gitlow wrote about the impact of his teenage exposure to Socialist oratory at the Frederick C. Howe Forum at Cooper Union; in unpublished biographical notes, he described a rally where Socialist leaders Mother Jones and Ben Hanford spoke. Their talk of class conflict in "the mines, the wheat fields, the fisheries, the hobo jungles and the lumber camps" began a romantic fascination with the Industrial Workers of the World that eventually led Gitlow to form a friendship with Big Bill Haywood. "I left the meeting convinced that in the end, Socialism would be victorious."

Left from the Start

American Socialism grew as one reaction to the rapid expansion of industry in the late nineteenth century. As a response to the rough edges of the free market, it was dwarfed by Populism and Progressivism, both of which found their way into the two major political parties. But Socialist thinking did find fertile ground among the largely eastern European Jewish immigrants on the Lower East Side of Manhattan. This was a match made in Marxist heaven — a combination of crowded and difficult living and working conditions and an immigrant community predisposed to dissident and leftist ideas.

Crusading journalist Jacob Riis helped create the lasting portrait of the Lower East Side: crowded, unhealthy tenements, with as many as a thousand people per square mile in the most populated blocks. More than 2,000 people lived in the two-acre area around the Gitlow apartment on Cherry Street. Some tenements doubled as workplaces for the nearly 100,000 who worked in the garment industry. Clothing manufacturers would subcontract work to individual employers, who would then hire recent immigrants to produce garments in tiny work spaces. It was the largely female garment industry on the Lower East Side that led to the popularization of the term *sweatshop*. The work was demanding, unregulated, and underpaid; the whole purpose of the system was to drive wages as low as possible. There was a constant influx of newly arrived immigrants (greenhorns) who could be employed cheaply. Theodore Roosevelt, then in his most Progressive period, was moved by what he saw and called for the government to intervene, writing, "We cannot as a community sit in apathy and permit these young girls to fight in the streets for a living wage and for hours and conditions of labor which shall not threaten their very lives."

These conditions, particularly among a population of immigrants who — like Louis and Kate Gitlow — had fought political battles in their former countries, were certain to create a left-of-center political culture. The Socialist *Jewish Daily Forward* reached a circulation of 200,000, the largest of any Socialist publication in the country. What is often called the Jewish Labor Movement was centered in the clothing industries and contained the most left-wing unions in the country. Teddy Roosevelt received a substantial number of votes for president from the Lower East Side, as did William Randolph Hearst in his early Progressive campaign for mayor. Meyer London, a Socialist Party candidate for Congress, drew a third of the vote in 1910 and then won a seat in 1914 — and this was before the United States' entry into World War I increased the Socialist vote total and sent Ben Gitlow to the New York Assembly.

The February Revolution in Russia that deposed the czar was

understandably popular with these eastern European immigrants. But initially, the October Revolution that brought the Bolsheviks to power was popular as well. Abraham Cahan, Socialist editor of the *Daily Forward*, would soon be a fierce opponent of the Bolsheviks, but at first he established a policy that his paper would carry no criticism of the October Revolution. Others were even more enthusiastic. The Communist *Freiheit*, a Yiddish-language daily, never reached the circulation of the *Forward*, but at 22,000 it outsold the Communist Party's signature paper, the *Daily Worker*. Socialists and Communists would become mortal enemies within just a few years, and throughout the 1920s and 1930s they battled for leadership of New York's garment industry unions. But in the beginning, a shared impulse – that the path to justice in Russia and America turned leftward – motivated support for both.

The leftist backdrop of the New York Jewish immigrant community led Max Eastman to write, in an introduction to Gitlow's second book, that Ben's early and active entrance into Socialist politics was "a mere matter of course." Gitlow himself noted many years later the socializing effect this political culture had on him and his three siblings: "The socialist phrases [we] heard sank deeply into [our] young impressionistic souls." What was not inevitable was that this exposure to immigrant Socialism would lead to the magnitude of his later involvement. Of the four Gitlow children, only his sister, Bella, joined Ben as an active participant in Socialist Party politics, and only for a brief period around the time of World War I. She remained a Socialist for many years – a stance at odds with her brother's – but was not active. (She reunited with Ben politically when they both became conservative anti-Communists in the 1950s.) His older brother, Samuel, became a doctor, served as president of the Bronx County Medical Society, and spent five years as a captain in the Medical Corps Reserve. His younger brother, David, became a pharmacist and moved to California.

But Ben Gitlow then and throughout his life gravitated toward large, encompassing theories, albeit very different theories at different points in his life. He described himself during his high school years as "a normal American boy popular among students" who excelled at sports, yet his main pursuit was the discussion of "Philosophy, Religion, Socialism, [and] Anarchism," which he was exposed to at Cooper Union. "I would turn over in my mind the things that left an impression upon me. In my mind would be the faces of those whom I had seen and heard, men unnamed, of unrecorded fame, who had kindled in me a spark of affection and admiration for them, men who might have given me a feeling for the world as it was and as it might be."

It is difficult to find a constant in his life of dizzying and perilous turns, but there was this: he never stopped trying to understand and act on the broadest questions confronting humankind. He wrote to his wife Badana from Moscow in 1927, "Books are to the mind what plows are to the earth." The flip side of his inclination toward sweeping theories of world events was disdain for those who did not share his passions. On his way to Chicago for a meeting of the Central Executive Committee of the Communist Party, he wrote to his wife about some businessmen he had encountered on a train. What bothered him most was not any political view they expressed or what class they represented but the smallness of their world.

I could not help but hear the conversation of true American petty [*sic*, or irony] bourgeois gentle-men from Westchester County. I thought Badana that I was in another world. One was such a golfing enthusiast he had so transformed his living room that he could play golf in it in the winter. . . . They talked quietly in mono-tones, seldom smiled, and looked bored. There was not one bit of color or appreciation of beauty in anything they had to say.

Pre-Bolshevik Socialism

Gitlow joined the Socialist Party in 1909, the first American-born member of the Harlem branch. His main practical work in those early years was with labor unions. After graduating from Stuyvesant High School, he worked in a variety of jobs, including as a clothing cutter, as a law clerk, and in a department store. In the last of these, he led a successful organizing campaign and became the first president of the Retail Clerks International. The *New York Times* published a letter he wrote for the union in 1915 on behalf of a state minimum wage bill for women. An associate in his early Communist days noted Gitlow's passion for — almost preoccupation with — the labor movement. "Gitlow never talked about anything but his union. . . . Whatever [he] started with, he would wind up on the subject of the union." That writer's husband was the leader of a contentious Communist-led textile strike in Passaic in 1926, and she noted that of all the party leaders, Gitlow was the only one who actually visited the site of the strike. Gitlow's son described his father's oratory as "inflammatory . . . a blood-curdling crescendo to rouse workers when he was a labor leader." Gitlow's passion for the labor movement survived his later turn to anti-Communism, and in 1939 he chose to begin his lengthy testimony before the House Un-American Activities Committee (known popularly as the Dies Committee) by reaffirming that commitment: "I have been in favor of trade unions all of my life, and I started my activities in the labor movement by organizing a trade union."

As a bright, dedicated young activist and a rare native English speaker, Gitlow quickly assumed a leadership role in the New York Socialist Party; he became a city branch organizer in 1912 and was elected to the party's Executive Committee. In 1912 he also became the campaign manager for Nicholas Aleinikopf, a Socialist candidate for the New York State Assembly and the man who had taught his father English. Aleinikopf lost, but that was a prelude to Gitlow himself winning a seat in the assembly in November 1917, representing the Bronx. In a three-way race, Gitlow received about 4,000 votes; Democrat Robert Mullen, 3,100; and Republican William Wachtel, 2,400. He was one of ten Socialists elected to the assembly that year in a surge of Socialist voting influenced by the party's opposition to American entry into the war.

The Socialist campaign platform was sweeping: an end to night work for bakers, an end to "occupational diseases," municipal ownership of public utilities, and an end to capital punishment. The reality of a Socialist assemblyman was quite different, especially for those who, like Gitlow, were moving rapidly leftward in response to world events. His fellow Socialist representative from the Bronx, Louis Waldman, described Gitlow's legislative input in a 1919 speech with Gitlow seated just a few feet away:

A bill comes before the House. The bill concerns those who sent

Gitlow to the Assembly. Ben Gitlow says . . . that we will have nothing to do with the legislation introduced by capitalist representatives. And he delivers a speech saying, "Your system is rotten. It is no good. The workers are not going to be benefited by your bill." A while later another bill comes up. Gitlow gets up and goes through the same performance of telling the capitalist legislature its worthlessness. The first time Gitlow speaks thus, he is a novelty. The second time . . . he would be considered a joke. The third time, he would be treated as a nuisance. Ben Gitlow having been in the legislature ought to know what I am saying is true.

Gitlow introduced several bills of his own, dealing with education, mothers' welfare, and state employees' salaries; none made it out of committee. Most intriguingly, he proposed a bill that would have modeled the state's protection of speech rights on the First Amendment. Had it passed, it might have changed the arguments in his later trial and appeals. Gitlow probably would not have quarreled with Waldman's caustic description of his role in the assembly, a body he saw mainly as "a bigger and better rostrum."

The inequalities in turn-of-the-century capitalism were at the heart of the early Socialist appeal, and they were certainly what initially attracted Gitlow to Socialism. But it was opposition to World War I that came to define the Socialist Party. Gitlow's campaign for state assemblyman in 1917 emphasized the Party's antiwar and anticonscription messages. The platform of New York Socialists localized war issues, advocating an end to the state conscription law, to compulsory military training in schools, and to the use of child labor on farms for the duration of the war. The leader of the party's legislative group, Abraham Shiplacoff, cleverly intermingled state, nation, and the two major parties: "To glance at the laws placed on the statute books of this State, one would think that the Republican Administration in Albany was presuming to teach the Democratic Administration how to conduct the war."

On a national level, opposition to American entry into the war both energized and isolated the Socialist Party, pushed it to the left, and led indirectly to the split that eventually created the Communist Party. Liberal reformers, whose previous positions had often overlapped with those of the Socialist Party and provided it with broader support, generally saw the war as a progressive venture and distanced themselves from the Socialists; a small group of members with similar views left the party. Unlike the European Socialist parties, almost the whole American Socialist leadership opposed the war in some form. Older, established leaders such as Eugene Debs tended toward pacifist language with a "class" twist: "Gentlemen, I abhor war. . . . When I think of a cold glittering steel bayonet being plunged into the white, quivering flesh of a human being, I recoil with horror." "Capitalism makes war inevitable. . . . Let us show the people the true cause of war." That was enough to draw a twenty-year jail sentence, but it was not enough for the young Turks who wanted the war condemned in more explicitly Marxist terms. Gitlow's version was "a capitalist shambles for imperialist profits."

Tectonic plates were shifting on the left. The war and America's eventual participation in it sharpened the already growing Left-Right tension among Socialists. That rift predated America's involvement in the war; the first gathering of a left-wing group within the Socialist Party took place in Brooklyn in January 1917 and was led by soon-to-be-monumental Russian figures Bukharin and Trotsky. Gitlow, still being something of a Debsian Socialist at that point, did not attend. But several people who were there would become prominent first in the Socialist Left Wing and then in the creation of American Communism less than a year later, including Louis Fraina, the principal author of the treatise that sent Gitlow to jail. When the Left Wing was launched, it proposed that the Socialist Party adopt as its slogan for World War I, "No truce with the ruling class! . . . War against capitalism. On with the class struggle!"

Red's Dawn

Then, into that simmering mix of war and leftward drift came news of the October Revolution in Russia. To leftists, this combination of war and revolution seemed to herald a turning point in history. The carnage of World War I was an example of the cataclysm of inhumanity that Marxists had always predicted capitalism would deliver. After the darkest hour came the dawn — the arrival of the first Socialist nation, the "Red star over the new Bethlehem," in Gitlow's rapturous words. This Christian phrasing from the Jewish Gitlow helps illustrate how the Bolshevik revolution electrified the left-leaning world. He later described his first reaction: "I deduced from the war that brutal force and violence were the final arbiters, and concluded that Socialism would come as a result of revolution in which the masses would use force and violence in overthrowing their oppressors. . . . The Bolshevik Revolution gave the Left Wing Socialists the program they were looking for."

That intoxicating combination of war and revolution was overwhelming proof to the Left Wing Socialists that their time had come. They had always believed — as Marxists generally do — that they had an appointment with history. But now history had actually appeared before them in the form of the October Revolution, verified in first-hand accounts by Left Wing leader John Reed, who was back from watching it unfold. It was irresistible. Gitlow, as one of the Socialists moving rapidly leftward, saw the events as the fulfillment of a prophecy: "The Revolution was on the march. We could not lose time. We had to march with it."

Gitlow was defeated in his bid for reelection to the state assembly in the fall of 1918, a result of the arithmetic of ordinary politics rather than the movement of apocalyptic historical forces. In the 1917 election, votes in the Bronx district he represented had been divided among Socialists, Democrats, and Republicans, permitting Gitlow to sneak in with a narrow plurality. But in the 1918 election, the two major parties united behind a single candidate to prevent a Socialist victory; Gitlow lost, even though he received more votes than he had in 1917. There is no mention in any of his public or private writings of this reelection campaign or loss; it was simply not at the center of his attention. His preoccupation was clearly the political battle inside the Socialist Party and, specifically, the movement toward creating an organization in America modeled on the Bolsheviks.

The Socialist Left Wing held a national meeting in New York on June 21, 1919. Gitlow was elected to the National Council, along with several others who would later be tried with him in the criminal anarchy cases: Isaac E. Ferguson, Jim Larkin, and Charles E. Ruthenberg. These American Bolsheviks-to-be moved out of the Socialist Party in a series of splits ending in the late summer of 1919. Gitlow, Reed, and Larkin were among those who stayed in the Socialist Party until the end (that is, until they were expelled) and then formed the Communist Labor Party; Ferguson, Ruthenberg, and another future criminal anarchy defendant, Harry Winitsky, left earlier and formed the Communist Party of America. What divided the Left Wing from the mainline Socialist leadership was not whether the Russian Revolution was a welcome event—almost every Socialist leader initially agreed that it was. The question was whether the Bolshevik organizational form and insurrectionary path to power constituted the Socialist key to the capitalist lock. Many in the Left Wing became convinced that the Leninist model—a tightly organized cadre of professional revolutionaries with a high degree of ideological unity—was a universal formula. In other words, the breakup of organizations over relatively small differences, which looks counterproductive to the naked eye, is actually the prescription for success. Divisions were simply an outgrowth of Lenin's logic of strengthening by splitting. Two Communist parties were created in the fall of 1919—one day and two blocks apart.

Unsurprisingly, then, the June 21 meeting of the Left Wing did not produce a unified course of action. But it did produce a single policy statement, called the "Left Wing Manifesto." There had been two earlier versions, published in the *Revolutionary Age* on February 8 and March 22. The final version was published on July 5, 1919, by which time the paper had moved to New York, and Benjamin Gitlow was listed as its business manager. These three versions, appearing within just five months, demonstrated the pace of the leftward march. The February 8 manifesto denied that secession from the Socialist Party was being contemplated; the final version mocked anyone who did not split. The July 5 manifesto called on Socialist Party members to repudiate the "moderate, petite bourgeois socialism" of the party leaders, as opposed to "the uncompromising proletarian struggle for socialism." Whereas the first version asked why European Socialists were supporting their governments in the war, the March version demanded that all Socialists support Lenin's slogan of turning the imperialist war into a civil war. The first praised activity by labor unions, through which revolutionaries could teach "solidarity and class consciousness"; the final version called for dual unions—that is, splitting from the mainstream labor movement "corrupted by imperialism" in order to engage in "the mass political strike against Capitalism and the state."

The theme of the final July 5 manifesto was that the Left Wing had to create an organization based on the lessons of the Russian Revolution, as popularized by the Bolshevik leadership. The Socialist goal had to be "to destroy the parliamentary state and construct a new state of the organized producers which will function as a revolutionary dictatorship of the proletariat." The primary vehicle would not be legislative measures such as those Gitlow had supported in the New York Assembly but "mass action," particularly the "political mass strike." The final version of the manifesto gave as an example of mass action the recent general strikes in Seattle and Winnipeg that had featured "striker-workers trying to usurp the functions of municipal governments."

> Revolutionary Socialism adheres to the class struggle because through the class struggle alone — the mass struggle — can the industrial proletariat secure immediate concessions and finally conquer power by organizing the industrial power of the working class. . . . The proletarian revolution and the Communist reconstruction of society — *the struggle for these* — is now indispensable. This is the message of the Communist International to the workers of the world. . . . The Communist International calls the proletariat of the world to the final struggle!

———

The Empire State Strikes Back

The intended audience of the manifesto was those on the Left whose lives revolved around debating and importing the lessons of the Russian Revolution. Written in transliterated "Bolshevise," the "Left Wing Manifesto" was unreadable to those who were not already committed. And even some who were committed had problems with the document. Gitlow and several others were genuinely critical of the writing as stilted and doctrinaire, both well-known tendencies of its author, Louis Fraina.

But the manifesto did have one very interested non-Socialist reader — Archibald Stevenson, a New York lawyer who had previously worked for the Bureau of Investigation and military intelligence and was an avid consumer of revolutionary literature. In 1919 Stevenson was instrumental in the formation of the New York Joint Legislative

Committee Investigating Seditious Activities, commonly called the Lusk Committee after its chairman, Senator Clayton Lusk. The task of the Lusk Committee was to "investigate the scope, tendencies, and ramifications of . . . seditious activities and report the results of the investigation to the Legislature" and, as added by its chairman, "to take such action, both preventative and constructive, as seems necessary for the protection of our institutions, and the persons and property of the citizens of the state." Lusk was a first-term state senator who had little understanding of leftist politics but recognized a political opportunity when he saw one. To make up for his lack of knowledge, he relied heavily on Stevenson, the committee's special counsel and an expert on Bolshevism. Stevenson decided that the various left-wing organizations could be prosecuted under New York's criminal anarchy law. In the 1919–1920 "Red Scare" period, more than thirty states passed some version of an antisedition law, but the New York law had been on the books since 1902. Although it had never been used, Stevenson described it in the Lusk Committee report as the potential legal centerpiece for a counterattack against leftist organizations: "Soon after this Committee was organized, it became apparent that the Criminal Anarchy statute of this state was being constantly and flagrantly violated."

The Lusk Committee took on an unusually aggressive investigative role for a legislative unit. Using the rationale that it was assisting prosecutors in preparing cases, it obtained search warrants for raids on its targets, including Soviet quasi-ambassador Ludwig Martens, whose unofficial bureau was in New York City; the Socialist-led Rand School; and the local offices of the Industrial Workers of the World and the Socialist Left Wing. Assistant New York Attorney General Samuel Berger's words of praise for the Lusk Committee raids demonstrated its essentially prosecutorial function: "The important part of these raids is that they *struck at* the source of radical propaganda [emphasis added]." The raids confiscated what the committee described as "revolutionary, incendiary and seditious written and printed material," as well as other threats to the social order; this included "a number of immoral books" that, "judging by the well-thumbed appearance . . . particularly appealed to the patrons of this library." The Lusk Committee's four-volume final report was almost laughably padded with lengthy and pointless excerpts from American

Socialist literature and the public statements and constitutions of European Labor parties.

There was little legislative result. The New York legislature enacted two noncontroversial Lusk Committee suggestions regarding the extension of educational opportunities for immigrants, based on the assumption that more education would counteract the Socialist leanings of European immigrants. It also passed two more significant bills recommended by the committee: one requiring a loyalty oath for teachers, and one requiring that schools be licensed by the state (this was aimed at the Rand School). Governor Al Smith vetoed the two school bills on the grounds that it was "unthinkable in a representative democracy, [that] there should be delegated to any body of men the absolute power to prohibit the teaching of any subject of which it may disapprove." When Smith lost the governorship in 1921, the legislature repassed the bills, and new Republican governor Nathan Miller signed them into law. The New York teachers' union challenged both laws in court, putting their implementation on hold. But before there could be a ruling, Smith was reelected, bringing with him a new Democratic majority as well as a diminished public interest in the Lusk Committee's goals. Both laws were repealed in 1922.

If the legislative effect of the Lusk Committee was minimal, its role — and that of Archibald Stevenson — in instituting the criminal anarchy prosecutions was substantial. There were discussions between state prosecutors and the U.S. attorney general's office about whether to pursue New York's revolutionary groups under state or national law, and a strategic decision was made to use New York law. During World War I, leftists had been prosecuted under the national Espionage Act of 1917 and its amendments, sometimes called the Sedition Act of 1918. But after the war, Congress had rejected a proposal for a peacetime sedition law. Although creative prosecutors certainly could have found national laws under which to charge these revolutionaries, it made more practical sense to use an existing state law that seemed to apply directly. The attorney general's office was aware that national charges were problematic; in the more famous Palmer raids conducted two months after the Lusk raids, federal agents had been told to turn over any American citizens caught in the roundup of aliens to local law enforcement.

There was another obstacle to national prosecution. Secretary of

Labor William Wilson, at the prodding of Undersecretary Louis Post, ruled that the Communist Labor Party (which Gitlow had helped found), as opposed to the Communist Party of America (which Ruthenberg and Ferguson had helped found) "does not propose to use force and violence to accomplish the purpose." That ruling, vehemently protested by J. Edgar Hoover in his capacity as head of the General Intelligence Division of the Bureau of Investigation, prevented the deportation of dozens of aliens affiliated with the Communist Labor Party. The differentiation was not only unusually scrupulous but also, perhaps, clairvoyant—when Gitlow was expelled from the Communist Party a decade later, it was for the crime of "American exceptionalism."

November 8, 1919, was the second anniversary of the Bolshevik revolution, and its American supporters held celebratory events. Gitlow was in the middle of a speech in upper Manhattan when "about fifty police and detectives and operatives swooped down upon us in the name of the Lusk Committee. All the men present were lined up against the wall and searched for membership cards." Thousands were held initially, and forty-five were eventually charged. Gitlow took the arrest in the spirit of the aspiring American Bolshevik he was at the time: "When the examination was over, about twenty five of us were huddled into a patrol wagon and taken to police headquarters. But we were not a dejected crowd. We were in the best of spirits. We were, after all, revolutionaries ready to sacrifice all for the revolution, so that a mere arrest . . . was a trifling incident."

CHAPTER 2

"These Mad and Cruel Men"

The first stop on the path that ultimately led Ben Gitlow to the Supreme Court was his appearance with fellow defendant Jim Larkin in New York Magistrate's Court on November 13, 1919. The Magistrate's Court was headed by William McAdoo, former New York City police commissioner. These courts — sometimes known as "police courts" — had the dual function of arbitrating petty offenses and passing preliminary judgment on whether there was sufficient cause to proceed in more serious cases. Charles Recht, a frequent defender of accused leftists, represented Gitlow and Larkin at their hearing. He had appeared in front of McAdoo two days earlier on behalf of twenty-four others caught in the Lusk raids and quickly learned that McAdoo saw these defendants as combatants taken during hostilities rather than as alleged criminals whose guilt had yet to be proved. Among their exchanges was the following:

McAdoo: Our government is at war with Russia.
Recht: We are not legally at war with Russia. In fact, our troops have been withdrawn from Russia.
McAdoo: We do not recognize the government of Russia and to the United States, Russia is nothing but a state of chaos and anarchy.
Recht: We are not at war with Russia.
McAdoo: Who killed the 111 American soldiers whose bodies are being brought back from Russia?
Recht: I don't know.
McAdoo: Well, it was the Soviet Guards of Russia. Now let's get back to the law.

McAdoo concluded, "The Communist Party has declared a state of war against the United States . . . and the establishment of the Communist Party in the state of New York is the highest crime known to our law."

Five of Recht's first twenty-four clients pled guilty to unlawful assembly; charges against the rest were eventually dropped. Gitlow and Larkin were leaders, not underlings, and prosecutors prepared more serious charges against them — the *New York Times* headlined its article about the arrests "Drastic Penalties Planned for Reds." When they appeared in front of McAdoo on November 13, he raised their bail from $15,000 to $25,000. On November 14 McAdoo issued his statement of probable cause, sending the case to a grand jury. Of all the different venues where the prosecution outlined arguments against Gitlow, McAdoo's statement had the greatest sense of urgency.

First, the reason for the urgency: at issue was a deadly threat that had gone unrecognized by an unsuspecting public until it was almost too late. "This big-hearted, strong, young country . . . could not conceive that even a very small proportion of aliens hopelessly incorrigible to American civic influences . . . would fail to repay with loyalty and love, devotion to the institutions of a democratic state." And because of this public naïveté, there had grown a much wider circle of "parlor Socialists and pseudo-Anarchists who are looking for nervous excitement" and had some sympathy for the Communists' novel ideas, as well as "easy-going gentlemen" who could be hoodwinked by charges of official overreaction. (*Parlor socialist* was a widely used term of derision at the time, similar to *radical chic* in the 1960s.) McAdoo warned them not to be fooled: "In this projected revolution . . . the Jacobins are to swallow or to destroy the Girondists."

Then he dealt with a secondary issue but one that easily could have been central: that these men being charged under a criminal anarchy law were not anarchists. McAdoo noted that the "Left Wing Manifesto" "did not condemn" and was actually "most friendly and conciliatory" toward anarchism. In fact, these Communists may have been especially clever anarchists: "After the revolutionary Socialists have killed the state and suppressed or exterminated the bourgeoisie, they ask time to recover their breath and fill up the interregnum with a shadow of a government. He would certainly be an unreasonable anarchist who would not agree with this."

Here and elsewhere, prosecutors dealing with this issue presented the opposite of a standard critique of Leninism. The prosecution in this case portrayed Communists as closet anarchists, hiding behind the pretense that the end result would be an organized government. The more widely accepted view of Leninism was that behind its disposable egalitarian rhetoric was the goal of a totalitarian state. The prosecution did what lawyers generally do, which is to tailor an argument to fit the particular case. Here, the law specified criminal anarchy as the illegal doctrine. There was a bonus for the prosecutors in describing the defendants as anarchists. Six months prior to the Lusk Committee raids and arrests, there had been a wave of mail bombs sent to various governmental figures. The bombs had been the work of real anarchists, not Communists. But the confusion between the two enabled the prosecution to take advantage of the understandable fear created by the mail bombs.

Then McAdoo turned to what would be the central issue in these cases: how the words of the "Left Wing Manifesto" constituted a crime. Gitlow and the others were not charged with the commission of any overt illegal act or with conspiracy to commit an illegal act. Nor — and this is the constitutional controversy at the heart of the *Gitlow* case — were they charged with advocating that anyone else go out and commit an overt illegal act. The essence of the charge was this: the publishers of the "Left Wing Manifesto" advocated ideas that, if enough people agreed with them, might lead to illegalities at some point in the future. And far from being a mere historical analysis or prophecy that this *might* come to pass, the manifesto made it clear that the authors *wanted* it to.

The question the legal system had to determine was whether advocacy of this kind constituted a crime. More specifically: did the words of the "Left Wing Manifesto" violate New York's criminal anarchy law, and was that law a valid exercise of police powers when measured against the speech rights guaranteed in the New York Constitution? The additional question of whether the First Amendment to the federal Constitution posed any barrier to prosecution under state law was argued on appeal and was one of the central features of the ultimate Supreme Court decision. But McAdoo did not address it, explaining instead his more generalized notion of what speech rights meant and how they applied in this case. First, responding to the claim by Recht that the manifesto was protected speech:

Are we to lose ourselves in legal subtleties and nice disquisition and historical references and bury our heads in clouds of rhetoric about liberty of speech? Can these men openly state that they intend to destroy the state, murder whole classes of citizens, rob them of their property and then escape under the plea of liberty of speech. . . . Is the human mind entitled in civilized society to germinate poisonous and criminal thoughts and then scatter them abroad to beget anarchy, robbery, and chaos?

Second, on the argument that no overt crime had been alleged: the New York revolutionaries were "more dangerous to our civilization than the microbes of disease"; although both led inevitably to a bad end, at least diseases could be confined. This law, McAdoo observed, "is intended to head off these mad and cruel men at the beginning of their careers. It is intended to put out a fire with a bucket of water which might later on not yield to the contents of a reservoir." Then, to make sure that no one had missed his point (if that were possible), McAdoo announced his verdict before the case even went to the grand jury: "I am of the opinion beyond any doubt, reasonable or otherwise, that these defendants in their writing, concocting, . . . printing and circulation of the manifesto, are clearly guilty as charged in the complaint."

———

Wily Agitators, Illegal Acts

What McAdoo was describing, albeit in particularly lurid terms, was the then widely accepted legal basis for the prosecution of speech known as the "bad tendency" doctrine. If a speaker's words or writings can be read as encouraging others to engage in a course that might lead to illegal acts in the future, and if a jury finds that those acts (real or potential) are the reasonable, probable outcome of the speaker's intent, the words are just as punishable as the acts. Or more so — one well-known formulation of the bad tendency logic was Lincoln's rhetorical question, "Must I shoot a simple minded soldier-boy who deserts while I must not touch a hair of a wily agitator who induces him to desert?" The words lead inexorably to the acts and can be punished as though they were the same. Rather than being a specific test, the bad tendency doctrine was based on the commonsense reasoning that it would be foolish or even suicidal for a society to protect words that might lead to an increase in unlawful behavior.

The Lusk Committee report called the bad tendency argument "a well-settled principle of law." It continued: "Any reasonable man is responsible for the logical and reasonable consequences of his acts and utterances." The report contained lengthy excerpts from Socialist, Communist, and anarchist publications and platforms of all kinds and reached the same conclusion about all of them — that some reader would be influenced to commit illegal acts in furtherance of the outlined goals. "What more overt act is needed than the urging or counseling or advising another that organized government should be overthrown by force or violence? It is in this way that riots are started — the harangue, the rousing of the hot blood of the listener, the picturing of fancied wrongs, the appeal to the mob spirit, and then the mob in action."

That language was borrowed almost directly from the central rationale for the Sedition Act of 1798, and in fact, the Lusk Committee report explicitly praised that historically disreputable law. The proponents of the Sedition Act argued that a "mob working spirit" unleashed destructive passion that, once let loose, could not be countered by rational argument and must therefore be stopped in its initial stages. The Sedition Act was built around the same logic proposed by the Lusk Committee as the basis for prosecution — that protecting speech putting the constitutional order at risk was self-contradictory, even if the risk were not immediate. By the time it became immediate, it would be too late to prevent the evils. In the Sedition Act debate, Pennsylvania judge Alexander Addison said that the idea that the First Amendment should protect destabilizing speech was "a construction too absurd" to need rebuttal. "The experience of other governments and our own has shown us that libels on the power of the government naturally lead to insurrection. . . . [I]f the libels proceed, the obstruction of the powers of government may be too strong for removal." A congressional supporter of the Sedition Act made the same point more graphically: "Falsehoods [seditious libels] will have their effect, and even if afterwards contradicted . . . the truth avails but little. The poison is swallowed beyond the power of expulsion, even by the most powerful antidote." Or, as Abigail Adams put it, "Lawless principles naturally produce lawless actions."

It would be especially foolish to permit speech calling for illegalities when the authors of the words were devoting their lives to seeing that those results took place, as Gitlow and his associates certainly did. They were serious, dedicated, and committed Leninists, not misunderstood utopians. When Gitlow later repudiated his views of this period, he admitted he had been "engaged in treason and out to destroy the government of the United States." Seditious words can lead to seditious acts, so why should there be any protection for those words whose expression urges others to destroy the political order?

The bad tendency argument is not an unimpressive one. Of course, permitting prosecution for the bad tendency of words unconnected to overt acts could and did lead to silly actions by nervous or imperious political leaders, especially when the public was caught up in war hysteria. Several lengthy books have been written about World War I prosecutions for relatively mild dissent or offhand derogatory comments about the government or the war. But the New York criminal anarchy trials revolved around the essence of the bad tendency doctrine, not its excesses. The defendants were not reform-minded dissenters, and they were not little fish in the relatively small pond of American Communism. All but Winitsky were on the National Council of the Left Wing Socialists, and he was a New York leader. Larkin was even better known in England and Ireland for his militant union activity and radical Irish nationalism, and Ruthenberg was the leading figure in the eventual unified Communist Party until his death in 1927.

Archibald Stevenson, reviewing a book by civil libertarian Zechariah Chafee that was critical of the Lusk Committee and the bad tendency test, defended that doctrine (and his own actions) at length. "Under our form of government a man may entertain any opinion with respect to government or the prosecution of a war without violating any law or statute. Prosecutions . . . have been for the use of words or printed arguments urging actions which if carried out by the reader or hearer would have resulted in the commission of a crime." Stevenson then gave an example: if a man was at home and told his friend that a Negro charged with an attack on a white woman should be lynched – no crime. "On the other hand, if he went out in the street, gathered a crowd and expressed the same opinion, at the same time urging the excited citizens to go to the jail and seize the prisoner for the purpose of lynching him, he would then be advocating action which, if carried out, would constitute a crime."

The "Left Wing Manifesto" did none of these things, nor was it alleged at any of the trials that any of the defendants had spoken or written to excited citizens or told anyone to commit a crime. But the manifesto did, according to the Lusk Committee report, create "false ideas respecting government," and those ideas were actually more dangerous than the overt acts Charles Recht was demanding that the government demonstrate. To illustrate how seditious words could be more harmful than seditious acts, the report included an interview Stevenson had conducted at police headquarters with Dr. Max Cohen, a leader of the Left Wing Socialists and of the Communist Party of America. Cohen seemed to enjoy impressing Stevenson with his brazen candor. He admitted that to accomplish his goal of revolution, it would take force and violence, and he would be willing to say as much in court. "If I were to get on the stand and say that I don't believe in overthrowing the capitalist government, I would be lying." Stevenson extended to Cohen his "personal respect for your frankness," but he used that interview in the Lusk Committee report to demonstrate how seditious rhetoric was more dangerous than seditious deeds. "The advocacy of principles such as those enunciated by Dr. Cohen . . . constitute[s] a far more grave menace than that presented by bomb-throwing anarchists. The latter can much more easily be apprehended and his work, at best, is sporadic. But, the activities of Dr. Cohen are so widely diffused and so broadly prevalent that they constitute a very perplexing problem."

The New York prosecutors were as dismissive as Addison had been in 1798 of the argument that the Constitution protects those whose main purpose in life was to replace the American constitutional government with a Soviet system. In his opinion that sent the Gitlow and Larkin cases to the grand jury, McAdoo framed this issue in lively language:

A few years back if any one had said that in this year of grace 1919 there would be in the city of New York, known to the authorities, between seventy and eighty official headquarters of a criminal organization like this, well equipped with money and the rooms bulging with literature . . . he would have been laughed at. Nearly eighty recruiting barracks for this red army in the City of New York with thousands of members and apparently unlimited money, from at home or abroad. . . . To fail to enforce this law under the circumstances, would be on the part of public officials, judicial and otherwise, a species of treason against the state itself — at least the betrayal of a public trust.

The criminal anarchy trials would proceed, and the main evidence introduced would not be acts or speeches or even agitational leaflets. Although the prosecutors would introduce other evidence for context, the trials would turn to a great degree on one publication: the "Left Wing Manifesto." Their argument would be that, based on the logic of the manifesto, it was reasonable to infer that the defendants were advocating violence as a method of bringing about political change, thus violating the criminal anarchy law.

Target Practice

It was an unusual move to rest these important, high-profile prosecutions on a long, boring polemic intended to be read almost exclusively by other leftists. But the district attorney's office had a trial run for its theory. A Lusk Committee raid on June 21 at the New York headquarters of the Industrial Workers of the World (IWW) had turned up an anarchist newspaper written in Finnish called *Luokkataistelu* (Class Struggle). Archibald Stevenson was present during the raid and later testified at the trial that what had drawn his attention to this paper, among all the revolutionary IWW literature in the room, was that he had never run across it before. The editors, Gust Alonen and Carl Paivio, were indicted in August under the criminal anarchy law and went to trial in October, a month before the Lusk Committee raids on the New York Communists. Alonen and Paivio were Finnish anarchists, and both had arrived in the United States shortly before World War I; Paivio had jumped ship to stay in the country. They were midlevel IWW leaders and were involved more with other Finnish radicals than with the organization itself. In addition to editing *Luokkataistelu*, they supervised its production, financing, and distribution. According to a historian of the criminal anarchy trials, the assistant attorney general did not want to prosecute the other leftists until he had tried out this legal theory beforehand. So the district attorney's office got to test its plan of treatise-as-main-evidence and could begin with actual anarchists, eliminating the need to twist an anti-anarchy law to fit Communists.

The cast of characters in the Alonen-Paivio trial was almost exactly the same as it would be in the later trials. The nominal prosecutor was Edward Swann, but the bulk of the argument for the state was conducted by Alexander Rorke. The lawyers for Alonen and Paivio were Swinburne Hale and Walter Nelles, who were involved at various levels in all the criminal anarchy cases. The central connecting figure was Judge Bartow S. Weeks, who presided over all five trials and whose visibility in the Alonen-Paivio trial led to a death threat from anarchists. Prior to becoming a judge, Weeks had been a well-connected New York City lawyer and prosecutor, an active member of the American Olympic Committee, head of the New York Boxing Commission, and multiterm president of the New York Athletic Club. Weeks took his civic responsibilities seriously; he was "commander in chief" of the Sons of Veterans (of the Civil War) and a member of the Sons of the Revolution, and he had been a candidate for the state senate (he lost). Nelles, representing Alonen and Paivio in the preliminary hearings, noted that, on their first meeting, he found Weeks to be "extremely decent." Nelles recalled that after a bail hearing for Alonen and Paivio, Weeks called him to the bench "to explain to me further by an elaborate series of illustrations how impossible it would be for the world to subsist without the initiative and stimulation of private capital." Both of Nelles's characterizations may have been accurate, but he would learn that Weeks's deeply held belief in the danger of the defendants' ideas far outweighed his decency in shaping the trials. To an unusual degree, Weeks permitted lengthy conjectural debates about the nature of capitalism, Socialism, and representative government; he participated actively in those debates and more than held his own against the passionately committed defendants. Rorke for the prosecution focused on the illegal acts that, he maintained, flowed logically from the defendants' writings. Weeks appeared to believe that the more the defendants explained their ultimate goals and vision for social reorganization, the more evident the dangers and illegalities would be.

As with the later Communist defendants, there was no allegation that Alonen and Paivio had committed any overt criminal acts, and no evidence was presented that they had incited anyone else to commit illegal acts. The charge was advocacy of a kind that violated the criminal anarchy act. Rorke began by drawing a rigorous distinction between lawful radical dissent and criminal advocacy: "The theory of the People is that a man has a right to urge the overthrow of organized government in the country by lawful means and in the constitutional manner in which law is made and changed." But by publishing *Luokkataistelu*, the defendants advocated change by illegal means. Rorke knew that making this distinction was at the heart of his case, and he chose to emphasize the illegality of the means advocated rather than the ends (which, in the case of these anarchists, were not very clear anyway). He stuck to this distinction throughout the criminal anarchy trials, even when Weeks enthusiastically engaged the defendants in discussions intended to show that their proposed ends were criminal and that those ends logically necessitated criminal means. Rorke was trying to specify the kind of advocacy that might be considered illegal and imbue his case with a kind of commonsense logic, but that plan created a problem for him — although Alonen and Paivio and later the Communists predicted and *praised* illegal acts, they did not directly advocate them.

The prosecution's plan was straightforward — to demonstrate that *Luokkataistelu* advocated illegal means and that Alonen and Paivio were responsible for its production. Rorke's opening statement consisted largely of reading the newspaper's own revolutionary language to the jury: "It [*Luokkataistelu*] represents the fighting tactics of the extreme revolutionary side against the capitalist class. . . . There is no middle way or a way that is too revolutionary." In keeping with his attempt to specify the advocacy of illegal means, and as he would do with the "Left Wing Manifesto" in the Communist trials, Rorke focused not on the anarchist program but on specific phrases. Here, they were contained in an article entitled "The Activity of the Rioting Masses":

To get away from this capitalistic slavery — the government, we have to do this work in the only way possible, by mass action. . . .

The capitalists themselves call this in the English language Mob Action.

Don't show them any more friendship . . . but organize into mobs. Destroy everything which gets in the way of your aspirations and is property of your enemy.

Alonen and Paivio had not written the article, and the prosecution did not claim that they had. But once Rorke had introduced its content at the beginning of his opening argument, he defined his task as a simple one: "The people will endeavour to prove that the defendants caused this magazine . . . to be printed."

From that point on, the state's case — and a great deal of the defense's case as well — resembled a burglary trial: Who went to whom with what money? Who received material in the mail? Whose handwriting was on receipts? Was information coerced from the defendants by police strong-arming? There was discussion of alibis and aliases to support or rebut the claim that Alonen and Paivio were connected with the production or distribution of *Luokkataistelu*. Ida Ahoe, a young IWW member who had told the grand jury that Alonen had given her a stack of newspapers to take to IWW headquarters, left Rorke dumbfounded when she casually testified on the stand that she had lied to the police and the grand jury because she was tired and wanted to go home. "That was all made up out of my imagination," she claimed. The person who had actually given her the papers, she now said, was a "sweetheart" whose address, occupation, and height she did not remember.

But in spite of the ordinariness of the evidence, this was a trial of revolutionary anarchists. One way this manifested itself — in contrast with most of the later Communist trials — was in the occasional breakdown of decorum. Early in the trial, Molly Steimer, an anarchist convicted in the landmark *Abrams v. United States* case, refused to stand when Weeks entered the courtroom. He decided to let her behavior pass rather than "giving her an opportunity to martyr herself." Throughout the trial, Weeks and Rorke repeatedly admonished the defendants for indications of disrespect. When Ida Ahoe was asked why she had left mail addressed to *Luokkataistelu* with Paivio, even though she denied having ever heard of the paper, her response was that she thought he might be nicknamed *Luokkataistelu*. Weeks interrupted her answer to say: "I don't want you to be flippant with me, young lady." A little later they had this exchange when Ahoe claimed she could not recall what Alonen had said at a public meeting she had attended:

WEEKS: Don't you remember anything that you heard Alonen say?
AHOE: No.
WEEKS: When did you forget it?
AHOE: I never remember remembering it.

A similarly combative but more meaningful interchange took place when Rorke tried to get Alonen to explain the anarchist view that the *state* was owned by capitalists. Alonen pretended that the term referred to the New York State government. Rorke asked whether any other state governments were owned by capitalists, and Alonen dodged the question: "I don't know other states as well, so I will stick to New York State." Rorke took exception: "You think this is funny, I suppose?" Alonen's implausible narrowing of what anarchists meant by the *state* irritated Rorke, but it also highlighted a difficulty inherent in a prosecution based on the probable outcome of words. The meaning of the *state* to anarchists — as well as to the Communists whose trials followed — was both crucial and flexible. Alonen, of course, was being disingenuous; the *state* certainly did not mean officeholders in Albany as opposed to those in Sacramento. In its most leftist formulation, the *state* combines *government* and *owners* — or, perhaps more accurately, it makes them both subordinate elements of a ruling capitalist class. When Alonen was pressed on this point later in his testimony, he responded, "I mean the whole thing. The land and the means and the means of the good things in life."

But pinning down what Alonen and *Luokkataistelu* meant by the *state* was critical to the prosecution because the criminal anarchy law specified that advocacy of the overthrow of "organized government" was illegal. The word *state* did not appear. Since the article in *Luokkataistelu* that was central to the prosecution's case called the state "one of the fortresses of capitalism" that had to be attacked, Rorke had to argue that it meant the same as a call to overthrow organized government. It did, of course, but Rorke wound up in the ironic position of demanding that Alonen affirm the strictest Marxist position that the state was nothing but the executive committee of the capitalist class. "You have to overthrow the fortresses of capitalism before you conquer capitalism, isn't that right?" he asked. "And this government, according to you is a capitalistic government, isn't it? Yes or no, as a man of principle?" Alonen declined to respond to what amounted to an offer to convict himself in order to remain "a man of principle," and the malleability of the term *state* helped him do so. He relied on the distinction between elected government and private enterprise. "I understand that this is a capitalist society, but in this capitalist society is the people's government of the United States. That is the way I understand it. . . . The people want it. I always abide by majority rule. When the United States people want the government run this way, I submit and always have submitted, and never did anything else but talk something that could be better."

Unlike Alonen's claims that he had nothing to do with *Luokkatais-telu* and that the *state* meant New York, this was not a simple evasion. The IWW did not believe that majority rule actually existed, and members could say they supported real democracy without inconsistency. Also, unlike some of the upcoming Communist defendants, Alonen made no pretense of having a tightly defined set of principles. Weeks and Rorke may have felt that Alonen misrepresented radical anarchism, but the deduction they drew from the newspaper article— that, as a tool of the capitalists, the government would have to be overthrown—was no more logical than the one the defendant expressed. How should the reasonable, probable outcome of the anarchists' writings be determined? Weeks spoke directly to that question and, in doing so, illustrated one of the flaws of the bad tendency test: "Those who are to construe that language for the purposes of this case are the judge and jury." The defendants were not allowed to offer an interpretation of their own words. When Hale objected that witnesses should be permitted to offer their understanding of what they had written, Weeks cut him off and effectively ended the defense's argument: "That may be one of the difficulties out of which this alleged defense has arisen, that individuals have sought to construe language as it seemed to them."

That ruling made the verdict a foregone conclusion. Alonen and Paivio were convicted and sentenced to four to eight years in prison. Weeks thanked the jury, pointing out that although a radical paper published in Finnish might not appear on the surface to be a grave danger, "it takes a very small germ to create a deadly disease – a very little of such poison might destroy the entire body politic." Weeks had sparred with the defendants and defense witnesses during the trial about the meaning of law, the legitimacy of government, and the importance of private property. In his closing remarks to the jury, he revisited those issues with no attempt to maintain any semblance of impartiality: "What is a country without nationalism? What are the citizens without patriotism? How empty is a life without religion?" He continued, "These principles of the abolition of wages can mean nothing unless something is substituted for it. And so far as I can learn, none of these many-changing theories and doctrines have formulated for the future existence – along any livable lines." He thanked the jury for sending a message "to dreamers and others having unbalanced delusions that this home of democracy and this land of the free is no place for them to exercise their rhetorical effects."

This mention of "rhetorical effects" in his send-off to the jury illustrates the small role played by speech rights in the proceedings. At the start of his closing argument, Swinburne Hale had made a perfunctory motion to dismiss on the grounds that the criminal anarchy law violated the free-speech guarantee of the New York Constitution and the due process clause of the Fourteenth Amendment. Weeks swatted that motion away in his charge to the jury by citing what was then the consensus on the issue: "The punishment of those who publish articles which tend to corrupt morals, induce crime, or threaten organized society is essential to the security of freedom and the viability of the state."

But the interpretation of speech rights (which would become central in Gitlow's trial and appeals) resurfaced forcefully, if accidentally, in the final minutes of the Alonen-Paivio trial, after Weeks's last speech to the jury. Rorke had mentioned in his closing that Hale's heart did not appear to be in defending his clients, and Hale wanted it known that this was not so: "I am glad to have been able to appear for them in this court." Hale explained that his passion for the defendants was based on what he considered to be the real issue: "I cannot recognize the existence in a democracy of any crime called criminal anarchy, and as far as possible I shall test this statute." Weeks responded that he had suspected this was Hale's position, even though there had been almost no mention of it in the trial. Then he returned to the germ analogy: "But your theory was that it was better to leave the germ of the disease to float in the air in the hope that it might not reach any fertile soil . . . and it was better a few became infected than the germ carrier should be segregated. Our legislature thought otherwise."

That exchange would be repeated in substance when the Supreme Court decided *Gitlow v. New York* five years later. It also led to a humorous give-and-take a few weeks after the anarchists' trial when Weeks (without mentioning Hale by name) publicly suggested that any lawyer who "questioned the validity of a statute after it had been passed" should be disbarred. Hale responded playfully, pretending that Weeks was referring to Rorke, who was widely known to be an Irish nationalist and had advocated the use of violence in that cause to drinking partners. Hale made a magnanimous offer to defend Rorke against any movement to disbar him.

CHAPTER 3

Conviction by Inference

After a successful warm-up with the relatively harmless anarchists, the New York prosecutors turned their attention to the Communists arrested in November. From the perspective of the Lusk Committee and the district attorney's office, these people and their organizations represented a different level of seriousness. McAdoo had laid out the basic argument, citing the existence of "eighty recruiting barracks" and "apparently unlimited money." The shock of the Bolshevik seizure of power in Russia was the backdrop for these prosecutions. The defendants did not merely sympathize with the Soviet government; they extolled it with a religious fervor. Far from seeing the October Revolution as a response to Russian autocracy, they saw it as humanity's future and created a Leninist party (or two) to move America in that direction. The fact that they had almost no following? McAdoo's response was echoed at every level of the case: "Well-meaning gentlemen tell us that we should not interfere with the incendiary when he is preparing the torch, we should only apprehend him when he is setting fire to the building. This statute is a preventative measure."

The narrative for the prosecution was straightforward: crush this incipient threat before it spreads. The response on the defendants' side was more complicated. Court cases pose difficult problems, both theoretical and practical, for Marxists who are convinced that law is a fig leaf for capitalist rule. It would be both incoherent and unappealing to argue that rights in a bourgeois state are a sham and then demand constitutional protection. Communists try to expose the illusory nature of democratic rights in a capitalist system, so presenting an argument based on constitutional principles would be worse than useless; it would give credence to the capitalists' claims that rights are real and the law is impartial. When Socialist Party leader Eugene Debs was convicted of violating the Espionage Act—a decision that drew strenuous objections from civil libertarians — *Revolutionary Age* described the verdict simply as a by-product of the class war: "The constitutionality or unconstitutionality of the law matters not, what does matter is that the application of the law is a class act. . . . Bourgeois democracy is a fiction for class consumption."

For Communists, exposing bourgeois democracy and the meaninglessness of rights is easy — until they face serious charges themselves. At that point, they have to figure out how to combine that abstract view with something at least minimally self-protective in court. The solution to that problem became known as the "labor defense." It had very little to do with the actual labor movement. The strategy of the labor defense was to publicize a case as much as possible (labor being only one audience) as an example of class injustice and to hold protest meetings. This would — in theory — put pressure on the legal system to bend to popular outcry. Whatever the actual value of the approach — and publicity and fund-raising certainly have real benefits — the language of the labor defense permitted Communists to present legal arguments in court without appearing to be complete hypocrites.

Ben Gitlow's mother, Kate, headed the Gitlow-Larkin Defense Committee, whose mission was to "defend workers who are arrested and prosecuted by the government for acts in the interest of the working class." The criminal anarchy cases were not — and, by definition, could not be — about speech rights; they were about workers' interests (as the revolutionaries understood them). Leaflets distributed by the Defense Committee claimed that Gitlow was "In Prison for His Loyalty to the Working Class." They called him "fighting Ben Gitlow," class warrior, and described him as "physically powerful, mentally alert, always a force the masters feared."

Kate Gitlow's letters to her son in prison were full of stories of enthusiastic rallies and protests and vows of triumph in the end. "The Defense Committee held a mass meeting in New Star Casino," she wrote. "It was a big success and the hall was packed . . . the cheers were hearty and long for you and the other boys." At the same time, she must have had private misgivings about the practicality of the labor defense, because she also wrote a letter to an assistant district attorney with a mother's plea to help her son. She did not tell Ben about the letter, knowing he would not approve, and in fact, she worried that it was a betrayal of their revolutionary values: "My desire to help Ben and my conception of the class struggle conflicted with one another. What shall I do? I am fighting with myself. Maybe Ben will never forgive me for that step." Even Gitlow himself had doubts about the usefulness of the labor defense. Other party members who visited him in jail assured him that "long before my time was up, I would be freed by the revolutionary workers." Gitlow drily observed, "I felt that this was too optimistic a view."

Winitsky, in a speech to a defense rally shortly after he was released on bail, best captured these early Communists' views on legal and political defense:

> We are not going to shout "democracy"; we are not going to shout "justice"; we are not going to complain about the raids of the Lusk Committee. . . . We expect that thing and if we were not raided by the Lusk Committee, we would be very much surprised. . . . Comrades, the Communist Party has no plea to make. We do not ask for justice from the Lusk Committee. We expect no justice from the capitalist class.

But like Kate Gitlow, Winitsky hedged his bet: "Though it is true . . . that we expect no justice from the capitalist class, still we recognize that there are certain rights which we have and we are going to fight every inch of the way to maintain the rights we have." The defense would therefore be a balancing act, using the court as a forum to denounce capitalism and bourgeois justice while making use of "certain rights" that might enable their lawyers to keep them out of jail.

The defendants chose to be tried separately, and the prosecution decided that Gitlow's trial would be first. The prosecutors' reason for doing so seems clear. The centerpiece of the trial was going to be the "Left Wing Manifesto" published in the July 5 issue of *Revolutionary Age*. One task for the prosecutors would be to connect the defendant with its publication in some specific way, and Gitlow was by far the easiest connection to make. His name was on the masthead of *Revolutionary Age* as business manager, listed third behind Louis Fraina and Eadmonn MacAlpine. Neither of those men had been arrested in the Lusk Committee sweep; they were, in fact, out of the country. Fraina, probably the main drafter of the "Left Wing Manifesto" and blamed by all the defendants for its jargon-filled style, was attending meetings with Communists from other countries, first in Amsterdam and then in Moscow for the second meeting of the recently formed Third International, where he was joined by MacAlpine. That left Gitlow as the one person with an easily demonstrated connection to the manifesto who was still in the country.

There was no common strategy or coordinated approach to the trials, and the defenses turned out to be very different. Each presented a mix of legal argument and political proselytizing, determined to some extent by the personality of the defendant and by how much discussion of Marxism Weeks was willing to engage in (substantial, for instance, in the Ferguson-Ruthenberg trial). Gitlow's trial was an anomaly. There was a minimal effort to rebut the charges and a maximum of soapboxing, culminating in Gitlow's speech to the jury. In the other three trials, more attention was paid to examining and arguing over the evidence, and in some ways, they were more interesting. But Gitlow's trial was first chronologically and must be discussed first; the quick verdict and severe sentence influenced the decision making of the rest of the defendants.

Darrow Bearing Gifts

The shape of Gitlow's defense was, to some extent, an ad hoc decision made shortly before the trial. Up to that point, the legal work for all the defendants had been handled by left-leaning New York lawyers Hale and Recht. Recht had represented Gitlow and Larkin at their joint appearance in Magistrate's Court, and he handled jury selection in this one. But then Clarence Darrow showed up at the last minute to conduct the trial. This seems to have been a decision by Gitlow's party, since the defendant himself did not meet with Darrow until the night before the trial began and had not mentioned him in any previous letters from prison. Even though it wound up in the Supreme Court, this was not one of Darrow's better-known cases. His biographers barely mention it, and his performance in the trial was that of someone with a train to catch. Darrow had defended Marxists, including Ruthenberg, in other cases, and he told Gitlow there was little doubt about the verdict. "Oh, I know you are innocent, but they have the country steamed up. Everybody is against the Reds." What he heard from Gitlow made things worse. Gitlow wanted to use the trial for proselytizing. He "would not deny, but affirm and defend, every communist principle in the Left Wing program." That eliminated Darrow's ability to argue against a conviction by presenting the "Left Wing Manifesto" in a less extreme light and using ambiguities in its language to portray it as a call for reform. Gitlow wanted to testify that it did in fact call for an insurrectionary path to Socialism and for the expropriation of property without compensation and that he wholeheartedly endorsed those goals. That kind of testimony would not give Darrow much to work with, so he and Gitlow reached a compromise: Darrow would not put Gitlow on the stand, but he would ask the judge to allow his client to make a statement. Gitlow characterized Darrow's unenthusiastic endorsement of his request to speak to the jury this way: "Well, I suppose a revolutionist must have his say in court even if it kills him."

The trial began on January 30 and revolved around a single claim — that the "Left Wing Manifesto" advocated the overthrow of the government by illegal means, in violation of the criminal anarchy law. There were three lines of counterargument open to the defense. The first was that Gitlow was not responsible for publishing the "Left Wing Manifesto." That was the tack Alonen and Paivio had taken with regard to the publication of "The Activity of the Rioting Masses" in *Luokkataistelu.* The second was to argue that no crime had been committed; that is, that the words of the "Left Wing Manifesto" were just history and prophecy, not "advocacy," as the criminal anarchy law required. The third possible defense was that a law criminalizing advocacy alone, unconnected with incitement to illegal activity, was unconstitutional. The defense in the later trials used parts of each of these three arguments, in different proportions. But because of Gitlow's decision to use his trial as a forum to advertise his political beliefs, the first was completely off the table. Darrow stipulated very early in the proceedings that, as business manager, Gitlow was responsible for the article. The second line of defense was almost impossible because Gitlow would not give testimony that might soften or muddy up the implications of the "Left Wing Manifesto" (although Darrow tried to do that in his summary). So the only hope of winning the case was to demonstrate that the New York law ran counter to the country's free-speech traditions.

Rorke devoted most of his opening argument to demonstrating Gitlow's responsibility for the article, not anticipating that Darrow—who made no opening statement—would not deny it. The rest of his presentation focused on how the words of the "Left Wing Manifesto" advocated illegal acts and why these Communists were actually anarchists. When Rorke called his first witness—a printer who intended to testify that Gitlow had contacted him about printing *Revolutionary Age*—Darrow introduced his surprise stipulation: "So that it may save time, my client was the business manager and on the board of this paper, and there will be no attempt on his part to deny legal responsibility for it under the statute. . . . [W]e shall make no effort to deny the legal responsibility of this defendant for the publication."

Rorke and Weeks tried to make sure that Darrow was not leaving any wiggle room:

RORKE: Knowingly?
DARROW: Certainly knowingly.
WEEKS: With the defendant's knowledge?
DARROW: Yes.
WEEKS: He caused its printing?
DARROW: Yes sir.

There were fifteen questions from the court and the prosecution intended to test the breadth of the stipulation, and Darrow acceded to all of them, including an admission that Gitlow had negotiated with the printer for the publication of the July 5 *Revolutionary Age*, which contained the final version of the "Left Wing Manifesto."

But Rorke proceeded as though he had to prove Gitlow's responsibility for the publication anyway. Witnesses testified that they had seen Gitlow in the office where *Revolutionary Age* was delivered, that they had gotten checks from him, and that they had discussed with him the details of printing and delivering the paper. His sister, Bella Fruchter, testified under subpoena that she was on the staff of *Revolutionary Age* and that her brother wrote her paycheck. Darrow repeatedly pointed out that the defense had already admitted responsibility and there was no need for this kind of detail. At one point, when a prosecution witness proved to be incoherent about the details of the paper's printing, Weeks upbraided Rorke for putting someone who was unprepared on the stand. Darrow jumped in to state that he had no objection to the testimony because the defense was not contesting Gitlow's responsibility. Darrow raised serious objections to only two lines of questioning: Rorke's constant efforts to remind the jury that there were other criminal anarchy cases to follow (Weeks upheld the objections), and Weeks's insinuation that Gitlow was pocketing money owed to *Revolutionary Age* ("I'm afraid that your imagination is not as vivid or as broad as I thought, Mr. Darrow"). But his main goal was to move the prosecution's case along as quickly as possible.

Why did Darrow and Gitlow make these concessions, and why did Rorke proceed anyway? The second is easier: Rorke was on guard against tricks. After one of Darrow's many "we've admitted that, can't we move on?" objections, Rorke responded, "I am afraid of Greeks bearing gifts." But the simplest explanation for the defense strategy — that Gitlow's legal responsibility for the article was so obvious there was no purpose in denying it — is probably not sufficient. Gitlow clearly did not write or even contribute to the article. He was the business manager, not the editor. The actual writer of the article — Fraina — landed in a rival organization shortly after it was published. And Gitlow moved to a new newspaper, the *Voice of Labor*, motivated in part by his discomfort with the amount of bombast in the "Left Wing Manifesto." Darrow probably would not have won on the issue of legal responsibility, but he certainly had grounds to try. His lack of familiarity with the defendant and with the facts of the case may have contributed to his stipulations, as did Gitlow's refusal to sugarcoat his political views. It is likely that Darrow believed his only chance for acquittal was to convince the jury that the article posed no real danger, and the best way to do that — given that Gitlow wanted his moment in the revolutionary sun — would be in his own closing statement. So he sped things along to get there.

Most of the witnesses Rorke called to testify to what the defense had already conceded were reluctant Left Wingers who had been subpoenaed. The most overtly hostile was Rose Pastor Stokes. Stokes, who was also a Communist, was then in the process of appealing her own ten-year sentence for violating the Espionage Act (a case she won a month later). When asked whether she was a member of the Socialist Left Wing, she invoked the Fifth Amendment, a fact that Rorke referred to in his own summary to suggest that these party members lacked integrity: "Nobody remembers anything. And then pressed a little further—'I decline to answer on the ground that my answers might tend to incriminate me.'"

Rorke then turned to the task of showing how the words and ideas in the "Left Wing Manifesto" violated the criminal anarchy law. He began by reading the entire tract to the jury, interrupted only by his plea to Weeks to get Harry Winitsky to stop laughing. Apart from its bellicose and vaguely insurrectionary tone, there were two elements in the manifesto that the prosecutors in all four trials highlighted. The first was the Left Wingers' criticism of the moderate Socialists. The goal of the Left Wing during the split in the Socialist Party had been to rally those members who, unlike the moderate old guard, saw Bolshevism as the path forward. To that end, the manifesto was sharply polemical: "The Socialist Party not only repudiated industrial unionism, it still more emphatically repudiated its revolutionary implications, changing to petite bourgeois parliamentarism and reformism. . . . There can now be only the Socialism which is in temper and purpose with the proletarian revolutionary struggle."

Rorke used the moderate Socialist Party leaders as a foil, notwithstanding the fact that five of them were being expelled from their elected seats in the New York legislature (one from Gitlow's old Bronx district). His overall stance throughout the trials was that a person was free to advocate any system as long as the means advocated to achieve it were not illegal. Here, he pointed out that the "Left Wing Manifesto" attacked more traditional Socialist leaders such as Debs precisely because they advocated that Socialists use constitutionally provided parliamentary means to change the system. So, Rorke deduced, the manifesto must be urging illegal activity. Whereas the Socialist Party "believed in the form of government we have got in the United States," Rorke argued, "Gitlow, Ruthenberg, Ferguson, and the others [believed in] extra-parliamentary acts for the destruction, the conquest, and the annihilation of the government of the United States."

The second specific element from the manifesto cited by Rorke was its mention of the general strike that had taken place in Winnipeg, Canada, in May and June 1919. That strike began as an attempt to force union recognition and collective bargaining in the building and metal trades industry. It then expanded into a broader confrontation when employees throughout Winnipeg went on a sympathy strike. Many of the strikers were municipal employees, and basic services to the city were closed down, including firefighting and some police work. To avoid life-threatening situations, and probably also to maintain public support for the strike, the Central Strike Committee issued permits for limited work and required those employees to post a prominent red card reading, "Permitted by the authority of the Strike Committee." How could a strike in another country be introduced as evidence in the United States? Rorke offered it as the key to understanding the Left Wing radicals' game plan for this country. He read to the jury the manifesto's description of Winnipeg: "Strikes are developing which verge on revolutionary action, and in which the suggestion of proletarian dictatorship is apparent, the striker-workers trying to usurp functions of municipal government, as in Seattle and Winnipeg."

The prosecution made the strike in Winnipeg a living example of the illegal means and ends the manifesto advocated. Introducing testimony about Winnipeg permitted Rorke to do more than draw inferences from the logic of the manifesto; he could point out the actual conditions these revolutionaries wanted to create. The Winnipeg strike occupied more pages of testimony in the four trials than any other single issue. The strike was not particularly violent, but the aspect of the Winnipeg issue that was most interesting to the prosecution (and even more so to Weeks) was exactly the one that fascinated leftists: "striker-workers trying to usurp the functions of municipal government." This was not just a worker-employer class conflict; it was a proto-soviet, with striking workers taking over governmental tasks. A strike committee that ensured the provision of minimal levels of police, hospital, and health-inspecting services for humanitarian reasons might not seem sinister, but to the prosecution, it was the heart of the matter. It was a challenge to the deepest legal principle, the legitimacy of properly constituted authority. Weeks rejected defense objections: "This sort of strike did usurp the functions of the municipal government, to illustrate what these people mean."

The Winnipeg witness in the Gitlow trial was Major Furry Ferguson Montague. He had joined with other World War I veterans to do volunteer police work during the strike — a form of opposition because it was not approved by the strike committee. His testimony mainly described those who struck: telephone workers, postmen, railroad workers, milkmen, bread makers, hospital workers, water workers, and garbage collectors. The three daily papers ceased to publish and were replaced by the *Western Labor News Strike Bulletin*, which was issued daily and became, in effect, the city's official newspaper. Montague also talked about some of the burdens the strike imposed on the city: there was no telephone service for a month; ordinary citizens could not send telegrams; it was impossible to get gasoline; and, due to the garbage workers' participation in the strike, "I saw garbage stacked up in all directions everywhere."

But the prosecution had made a mistake in its selection of witnesses. Because Montague had no inside knowledge of the strike committee, he was not permitted to testify about who was causing what to happen. So, for instance, he could not say that the rationing of basic services was "permitted" by the committee or that other services were "forbidden"; he could only state that they were or were not offered. And although he testified that cards were posted on the businesses that were open, he was not allowed to say what was printed on the cards. Weeks did his best to overcome the prosecution's mistake, which prevented the "usurp the functions" discussion he was most interested in, by getting Montague to say that many of the struck services were licensed by the city government and that no lawful authority had revoked the licensing procedure. But in the end, the import of Montague's testimony was largely that the strike had created a mess in Winnipeg, and the writers of *Revolutionary Age* loved it. The flimsiness of the Winnipeg evidence was one possible line of attack for Darrow, but he did not pursue it. His objections were limited to demonstrating that the purpose of the strike had been to force the city to engage in collective bargaining.

"I Ask No Clemency"

At the conclusion of the prosecution's case, Darrow produced his second surprise: "My impression is now that we will rest as it is. The defendant wishes to make a short argument to the court." Weeks immediately ruled that Gitlow would be allowed to do so: "It is very unusual to allow a defendant who has not taken the stand to address the jury . . . but I do not feel it should be refused at this time." He imposed only one constraint — that Gitlow had "no right whatsoever in his address to make any statement whatever that is not based on the testimony and evidence in this case." Others who have written about the trial speculate that Weeks believed Gitlow would hang himself by antagonizing the jury. That is plausible, since it is exactly what happened. But Weeks never gave a reason for his decision, and there was no objection from Rorke to force an explanation. Nor was it out of character for Weeks to permit an airing of Gitlow's views. Although none of the other criminal anarchy defendants made a speech of exactly the same nature, there were other lengthy presentations on the principles of Communism, and far from reining in those discussions, Weeks seemed to egg them on.

In his summary, Rorke referred to Gitlow's fifteen-minute speech as "brazen," and it certainly was that. Within the first few minutes, Gitlow declared, "I am a revolutionist." But he also tried to communicate in more understandable language what the "Left Wing Manifesto" had said in Leninist jargon. Without repudiating any of the principles of the manifesto, Gitlow repackaged them, using imagery drawn from the IWW, his first leftist love. He asked the jury to imagine John D. Rockefeller in the Sahara Desert with all his wealth piled up beside him in gold. "Do you think that gold would be valuable? John David Rockefeller could stand there, look at these mountains of gold, see them towering to the heavens and not get something to eat." When describing what the dictatorship of the proletariat meant, he offered the IWW vision of social reorganization. "You have a form of government that is based on representation of industry. . . . The men in the shoe industry vote as shoe workers and choose their representatives to the council in the government[,] and the national government . . . is the representative of the working class."

This was Communism as a form of industrial democracy. In capitalist enterprises, the worker "has no democratic control at all. . . . In Russia the democratic control of industry has been put into effect." The Socialism Gitlow presented in court was partly a more saleable version and partly wishful thinking. Gitlow had come to Communism through the labor movement and wanted workers' rights to be at the center of it. His depiction of Communism was probably a genuine reflection of his own thinking, but it was laced with notions drawn from pre-Bolshevik radicalism. With this unusual chance to outline his vision on a public stage, Gitlow offered a mix of Lenin and Big Bill Haywood.

But he made no effort to soft-pedal his revolutionary intentions or to present himself as a respectable reformer. "My whole life has been dedicated to the movement which I am in. No jail will change my opinion in that respect. I ask no clemency." In his later anti-Communist years, Gitlow never referred to this speech in anything but positive terms. Although after 1940 he did not support a word of the substance of what he had said in 1920, he continued to describe that speech as an act of courage and integrity (in contrast, by implication, to the approach taken by many of his compatriots in their trials). Weeks interrupted him eighteen times to insist that he confine himself to evidence already presented and eventually forced a premature end to his oration.

Gitlow's speech was certainly audacious, and his party circulated it in pamphlet form. But Darrow knew that if Weeks's plan had been to let his client antagonize the jury, it had probably succeeded. In Darrow's summary, delivered right after Gitlow finished, he did not refer to the speech a single time and in fact barely mentioned Gitlow's name at all. The central theme of Darrow's closing was to depict the charges against Gitlow in the familiar form of authority persecuting a heretic. "As long as men speak, they will talk a lot of nonsense and here and there some sense. . . . But it is one way of finding out the sense and nonsense – to let people talk." The men who promoted radical new ideas were dreamers and, he said, "I am for the dreamers. I would rather that every practical man shall die if the dreamer shall be saved." He tried to soften Gitlow's self-description as a revolutionary: "For a man to be afraid of revolution in America would be to be ashamed of your own mother." In his autobiography, Gitlow accurately described Darrow's summary as "one of his flowery appeals to the jury." Darrow invoked Walt Whitman, John Brown, and a variety of other "dreamers" to try to divert the jurors' attention from Gitlow.

No Clemency Is Offered

Thirty years after the trial, Rorke told an interviewer that he believed Darrow's closing argument might have swayed the jury. Given the number of times he referred back to it in his own closing, he clearly thought he had to counteract it. Rorke's summary was a lengthy and well-thought-out defense of the bad tendency principle and an explanation of how it applied in this case. Darrow had read portions of the manifesto to the jury and apologized if it put them to sleep. Rorke claimed that was a ploy: "The article, said Brother Darrow, shrewd and clever, will put you to sleep. Yes, but if you read it, the hair on your head will stand on edge." He tried in similar fashion to turn Darrow's concessions against the defense, arguing that the purpose of admitting so much had been to minimize jury exposure to the viciousness of the manifesto's doctrine. He countered Darrow's contention that the manifesto was simply history and prophecy by urging the jurors to think about Winnipeg. Rorke knew there was one link in the bad tendency chain that he needed to make clear — the connection between the manifesto and some future illegal act. Darrow had pointed out that nothing in the manifesto incited anyone to violence or unlawful action. Rorke admitted that there was no open endorsement of anything illegal, but, he claimed, that was because the manifesto had been written by men who were too clever to do that — by "learned minds who had experience with the law and who tried to set forth a crime in such a way that when 12 men sat in the jury box, they would be befuddled." He contrasted Gitlow with "some poor, illiterate, ignorant Finn," obviously referring to Alonen and Paivio. But the violence and other illegal means were right there in the manifesto if one read it carefully, Rorke argued. "If the logical inference of what [Gitlow] says is force, violence, or unlawful means, it is immaterial whether he uses the word 'force' or whether he has used the word 'violence.'"

Rorke seized on one innocuous-appearing example to illustrate his point. "There is one line there in that Manifesto that makes the blood in any man boil": that the revolution starts with strikes of protest — the "mass action" at the center of the Left Wing program. Political strikes would illegally deprive people of life-giving services, including fire and police protection, as they had in Winnipeg. Then the revolutionaries would turn to the real goal — seizing private property: "Expropriate them all in order that we may have our great Red Day." But that would lead directly to violence because, as Rorke observed, "How are you going to take their property away without murder?"

There was the connection: from the ideas in the manifesto to murder, by logical inference based on the reasonable, probable outcome of the words. The task for the jurors was simple: punish those responsible for the "Left Wing Manifesto" as though violence were a certain consequence. "You gentlemen are standing as sentinels of our present social structure. You are standing on the frontier that separates us from anarchy."

Rorke paid almost no attention to Darrow's defense of the manifesto based on speech rights. He knew that Darrow's contrast between advocacy and incitement had been rejected in a series of Supreme Court decisions in 1919, and he probably thought Weeks would dismiss that argument in his charge to the jury. He did. Darrow, knowing he could not win a constitutional challenge to the criminal anarchy law at this level, had requested that Weeks narrow the law in his charge to the jury: "Unless you find that the defendant intentionally put into writing language reasonably and ordinarily calculated to incite certain persons to acts of force or violence . . . you must find the defendant not guilty." Weeks declined: "It makes no difference whether the language was calculated to incite, if the language does advise, advocate, and teach the doctrine. If a man tries to do it and his powers of expression are not such as will incite the person to whom he addresses his remarks, that is not his fault. He commits a crime when he advises it."

Weeks did not respond to the "certain persons" element of Darrow's proposed charge, a formulation that would have protected speech addressed to a general or indeterminate audience, which was the case with the "Left Wing Manifesto." Weeks's charge in the area of speech rights was short and emphatic, the centerpiece of which was a formulation of speech rights by Justice Joseph Story eighty years earlier: "The Constitution places no restraint upon the power of the legislature to punish the publication of matter which is injurious to the standard of the common law. It does not deprive the state of the primary right of self-preservation."

The jury returned in about three hours with a conviction. Darrow, sure of a guilty verdict, had already departed, leaving Recht to handle Weeks's presentencing interrogation of Gitlow. Weeks asked repeated questions about the financing of *Revolutionary Age*, still seemingly determined to prove that Gitlow had embezzled money. In fact, the exchange demonstrated that Gitlow was an unusually meticulous and scrupulous bookkeeper. Weeks also showed interest in the fact that Gitlow had accumulated no property, and in his thank-you speech to the jury, the judge tried to make that seem nefarious: "A young man, 29 years of age . . . of full intellect, confesses that he owns no property. . . . Is that in harmony with the ideas of ambition and self-improvement, that those who come from foreign lands are expected to have?" (For dramatic effect, he construed Gitlow's native New Jersey as a foreign land.)

Weeks concluded by commending the jury for its "proper and just verdict": "You must have something substantial under you, or you cannot stand, and the substance in this country is the government. . . . [T]he lesson that has been taught from your verdict is one that will reach out and influence and save these misguided idealists who have allowed themselves to be carried away beyond their depth into the stormy waters of a would-be revolution."

On February 11 Gitlow appeared for sentencing. Rorke made a more melodramatic case for the seriousness of the offense than he had during the trial. Gitlow, he claimed, would "set up a hostile army, principally foreign born, and carry on war here on behalf of the dictatorship of the proletariat . . . as an ally of Lenin and Trotsky's government." Moreover, "the statutory penalty seems hardly adequate for one who sought to destroy the government . . . and annihilate our civilization." Neither Gitlow nor Recht made any plea for a reduced sentence. Weeks agreed that there was nothing the defense could say to mitigate "this most heinous offense" and sentenced Gitlow to the maximum of five to ten years at hard labor.

For their part, the American Communists and their allies saw Gitlow's defiant speech as their finest moment. The *Voice of Labor*, the paper Gitlow helped create after leaving *Revolutionary Age*, drew these conclusions: "The indictment and conviction of Gitlow is meant to intimidate those workers who are at one with the emancipated proletariat of Russia." Likewise, "the conviction . . . is meant to stay the onward march of the workers in this country. . . . It will have the opposite effect." Arturo Giovanitti, a left-wing poet who attended and reported on the trial, hyperventilated:

A finer specimen of manhood could not have been selected by the Communists as their first ambassador to begin negotiations for the capitulation of capitalism in its innermost citadel. Big, dark, wholesomely fleshy, he seemed to have been carved out of a huge granite rock by the sledge hammer of a master, with simple and mighty blows, without any whittlings of the chisel nor any pandering to the anaemic tastes of the fashions.

But the prosecution, both in New York and nationally, had gained a valuable tool by dismissing almost effortlessly the free-speech argument "so often and so wearisomely appealed to by the men and women who seek to overthrow freedom," as a *New York Times* editorial praising the verdict put it. The prosecution had convicted Gitlow for inferences in an article that he did not write, was not addressed to anyone in particular, and urged no one to commit any illegal act. There were more trials to go, but the major hurdle had been cleared.

CHAPTER 4

"Is This the Way to Fight Us?"

Although the next three trials offered variations on the themes of the Gitlow trial, they were not anticlimactic. Each had its dramatic high points, even though they all ended with the same verdict and sentence. They were more contentious than the Gitlow trial and posed more interesting legal and constitutional issues, yet the Gitlow verdict was chosen for appeal to the Supreme Court. Only brief and unilluminating comments exist as to why Gitlow's case was selected, and the only thing the record makes clear is that the decision to focus on his case was made after, not before, the trial. For instance, the head of the Civil Liberties Bureau, Roger Baldwin, never met or even communicated directly with Gitlow before 1921. The reason for selecting Gitlow's case may have been no more profound than the fact that it was first. But one thing is certain: it was not chosen because Gitlow's conviction raised the clearest First Amendment issues. That distinction went to Harry Winitsky, whose trial was the next one up.

Guilt by Membership

Winitsky, like Gitlow, had been born in America to Jewish immigrant parents, and he had come to Socialism in his early teens. Unlike Gitlow, his name did not appear on the masthead of *Revolutionary Age*. He was not a national officer of the Socialist Left Wing, and he had not even attended the founding convention of the Communist Party of America (CPA). He was simply a member of both the Left Wing and the CPA, although not an unimportant one — he was head of the Greater New York chapter. But Winitsky had no direct legal responsibility for the article used to convict Gitlow. The prosecution's argument in his case was that, as an active member of the CPA, Winitsky was responsible for all public statements of the party, and those statements, taken together, violated the criminal anarchy law.

His trial began March 19. William Bowers handled the bulk of the prosecution in this case, and he proved to be so inept that Weeks repeatedly upbraided him and ordered his questions stricken, sometimes even before the defense raised objections. The defense's approach was radically different from that in Gitlow's trial. Winitsky's lawyer was a sharp contrast to Darrow. William Fallon was a well-known defender of crime figures, including Arnold Rothstein, the gambler who had fixed the 1919 World Series. Fallon had no previous leftist defendants. He did, however, have a good record of getting hung juries through questionable means. (When he was later acquitted on a bribery charge, he told a reporter, "I'll never bribe another juror.") The CPA may have felt that Winitsky's case was winnable and that Gitlow's intransigence had unnecessarily sabotaged his chances. Fallon took a much more aggressive posture, objecting hundreds of times, including nine times in the prosecution's opening argument alone. Throughout the trial, Fallon and Weeks were openly antagonistic to each other, with only a bare pretense of civility — a sharp contrast to the somewhat cordial interactions between Weeks and Darrow.

To make a case against Winitsky, the prosecution needed one more link in the causal chain by which words came to equal illegal acts. Gitlow was responsible for an article that advocated illegal means to achieve its ends (according to the prosecution). Winitsky was one step farther away: he was a member of an organization that was responsible for such articles, thus establishing his own liability. This argument had some advantages for the prosecution. Rather than being limited to proving the criminality of the "Left Wing Manifesto," prosecutors could introduce into evidence the constitution and manifesto of the CPA, documents of the Third International, and even the constitution of the IWW, which the manifesto praised. The evidence linking Winitsky to the illegal advocacy in these statements was his status as a local leader of the CPA and his expressions of sympathy with its goals. So, for instance, a package he received from Ruthenberg containing material for a celebration of the second anniversary of the Bolshevik revolution became evidence of criminal anarchy, although it seems impossibly far from illegal advocacy. Likewise, the testimony of

Clarence Converse of the New York Bomb Squad was used as evidence: "I asked him [Winitsky] if he knew what the Manifesto contained, it was for blood and violence, and he said that he did and that if it was in the Manifesto, he stood for it." An undercover agent from Chicago reported in detail on banners, songs, and speeches at the organizing conference of the CPA, a meeting the prosecution acknowledged Winitsky did not attend. In response to Fallon's repeated and vehement objections to that testimony, Weeks explained the prosecution's theory of the case and the basis for widening the net of evidence:

> This defendant is charged with associating himself with a group of people who formed together for the purpose of advocating the overthrow of all government by force and violence. . . .
>
> How can you prove the purpose with which that group formed itself any better than to ascertain what was said when they were forming their organization? The purpose . . . may have been concealed in the written expression of their principles, under language which they understood [better] than the outside world.

As in the Alonen-Paivio and Gitlow trials, the state had to extrapolate the advocacy of illegal means from the goals outlined in the revolutionary rhetoric by demonstrating that the ends could be accomplished only by illegal means. But as in those earlier trials, that did not make an airtight case; both ends and means were subject to several interpretations. The "action of the masses" (which the CPA advocated), for instance, could be understood as legal strikes and protest marches. Fallon maintained that a call to overthrow "capitalism and capitalist government" was not another way of saying "overthrow the government of the United States." It was possible – by stretching concepts a little – to think of peaceful and lawful ways to expropriate property and scenarios in which violence might be purely defensive.

To demonstrate that illegal means were inherent in the platform of Winitsky's party, the prosecution leaned heavily on testimony about Winnipeg, as it had in the Gitlow trial. The principal Winnipeg witness this time was George Robert Lovatt, a policeman who had represented his union on the strike committee until he fell out of sympathy with the strikers' goals. Fallon objected strenuously to Lovatt's testimony. He argued that Winnipeg was mentioned only in the "Left Wing Manifesto," a document Winitsky had no direct relationship to; it was not mentioned in the program or the manifesto of the CPA – Winitsky's party. Weeks explained the relevance of the tenuous relationship this way: Winitsky belonged to a party whose program contained praise for political strikes and general strikes. How could the jury know what the CPA meant by a general strike? The answer: by looking at literature in which the party explained it. The manifesto mentioned "such a general strike as that in Winnipeg and Seattle." So Winnipeg was in.

When he was unable to get the whole subject excluded, Fallon proceeded to object to nearly every question and answer about Winnipeg, and in this he was more successful. Bowers seemed incapable of eliciting testimony that Weeks would let stand. Weeks at one point grew so frustrated with Bowers that he took over the examination himself ("See if we can make some progress here, gentlemen"). That led to even more vigorous objections from Fallon, who argued that the jury would inevitably see Weeks as a coprosecutor. "I do not think it is right. I do not think it gives the defendant a fair opportunity. I know I am reluctant when your Honor questions, because I know the spirit in which your Honor proceeds." After several other objections, Weeks came to the brink of holding Fallon in contempt: "The moment that I think you mean any disrespect, the Court will protect itself. . . . As I say, the Court would not permit you to object in any disrespectful way."

Lovatt testified to some of the same strike-related conditions that Montague had noted in Gitlow's trial, centering on everyday inconveniences – the absence of street cleaning, lighting, and garbage collection and the lack of hotel staff. Because Lovatt had been on the strike committee, the prosecution was able to get on the record his testimony that unions had been "ordered" to go on a sympathy strike and that businesses that remained open had received written permission to do so from the strike committee, which issued them red work permit cards (although Weeks would not allow testimony about what was written on the cards). That was the heart of the Winnipeg example for the prosecutors: strikers' organizations had taken over the proper functions of an elected government. Weeks's ears perked up when Lovatt mentioned in passing the existence of a "soldiers' parliament." That phrase intrigued the judge because it seemed to be evidence of the "soviet" direction of the strike. But it turned out to be nothing more than a pretentious name for a group of soldiers who supported the strike. Nevertheless, the prosecution's larger point was a fair one. The strikers and the strike committee *had* become the de facto governing body of Winnipeg for a short time – which is exactly why the "Left Wing Manifesto" praised the Winnipeg strike and pointed to it as a sign of things to come.

If Winnipeg was the prosecution's linchpin on the issue of illegal means, the most compelling moment in establishing Winitsky's connection to the CPA was the testimony of Jay Lovestone, a young but important party leader. (Lovestone and Gitlow would alternately be strong allies and bitter opponents over the next forty years.) Lovestone's testimony was so important to the prosecution that Rorke took over for the inept Bowers. The prosecution's goal was to tie Winitsky to the CPA in detail and establish that he was not merely hired help, as Fallon tried to paint him. Lovestone testified that Winitsky "sent out the letters, the literature, and the requests for money" and was responsible for "Party News," a column in the local Communist paper. The CPA had agreed on a program at its convention, and Lovestone brought it to Winitsky, went over it with him in detail, and worked with him to set up educational training for the local chapter. The tone of Lovestone's testimony was not friendly to the prosecution; his answers were curt and sometimes confrontational. In his summary, Rorke referred to Lovestone as "that witness we had to force on the stand." But he substantiated one of the important links the prosecution needed to make its case: Winitsky was not just a functionary; he was an active advocate of his party's principles. This was not merely an abstract issue. The case against Ferguson and Ruthenberg would ultimately be overturned on appeal based on the lack of proof of close ties between the defendants and the manifesto. If the prosecution had not succeeded in painting Winitsky as an active and knowledgeable party leader, he might have been able to take advantage of the same argument on appeal.

Like Darrow, Fallon called no witnesses. Also like Darrow, he used his summary to distinguish between advocacy and incitement. "There is not a word in the manifesto [of the CPA, not the 'Left Wing Man-

ifesto'] that directs anyone to do a particular thing." He admitted that
Weeks would probably instruct the jury that "the right of free speech
does not extend to the right of advocacy of revolution" (he did) but
said that the jury still "must find advocacy to do a particular act . . .
not to talk about, but to accomplish." Fallon was a little freer than
Darrow to transform his client's revolutionary rhetoric into a more
palatable populism, because Winitsky had not made a Gitlow-like
speech to the jury. Thus, the Communist program was transformed
into an argument for the progressive income tax and the Interstate
Commerce Commission, and Winitsky became one of a long line of
reformist economic crusaders protesting the unequal distribution of
wealth.

Rorke tried, as he did in all the trials, to draw a distinct line
between the right to speak critically and the advocacy of criminal
means. "A man in this country if he wants has the right to stand on a
street corner or in the halls and advocate the overthrow of the government . . . and he can do that legally. . . . But the moment that he
advocates the overthrow of our government by force and violence . . .
that means is in violation of this statute." But the only thing the prosecution had actually established was that to bring about the ends specified by Winitsky's party, it, and therefore he, must logically advocate
the use of force and violence. Winitsky's crime was being a member
of a party that stood on street corners and in halls and advocated revolution. Whether to remedy that defect or just to excite the jury,
Rorke added an element he had not used in his *Gitlow* summary — that
this Communist appeal was directed to uneducated people who might
be easily influenced to act on it differently than the speaker intended.
Rorke argued that William McKinley had been shot by "just such a
crack-brain who had gotten literature" and had become an uncon-
trollable carrier of class hatred. "What is more, we are going to take
the Negro, by Judas, we are going to take the Negro and stir him up."

In his sentencing speech, Weeks added to that line of thought: "the
weaker and more susceptible of your following are excited to the commission to acts of violence." As he sometimes did with startling insight
throughout the trials, Weeks accepted for a moment the premise of
the Communist defendant and asked him to look at the consequences:
"When you preach to the less intelligent people before you, that it will
be only a short time before the officers of this country will be inside

bars looking out at you, although for a short time you may be inside the bars looking out at them, how do you expect these less intelligent people to act? What must follow?"

The "must" in Weeks's final question was a single-word synopsis of the bad tendency doctrine. Winitsky's membership in the CPA equaled the McKinley assassination. Weeks, characterizing Winitsky's activities as "very close to treason," sentenced him to five to ten years—same as Gitlow. On the May Day following his conviction, Winitsky sent this message from jail: "I have been sentenced to prison for having been a member of the Communist Party. . . . If it is a crime to advocate the destruction of the capitalist class . . . then I have the honor of pleading guilty." That was the underlying problem for the defense, which made Fallon's talents useless: in that era, "to advocate the destruction of the capitalist class" *was* a crime.

————

The Catholic Marxist

All five defendants in these trials were, to varying degrees, well known within American Communist circles. But those circles lacked a wide radius. The only defendant whose reputation extended farther was Jim Larkin, next up for trial. Larkin had been so well known as a labor leader and Socialist in Ireland that *Larkinism*—the use of widespread sympathy strikes and general intransigence toward employers—had become a common term. Larkin came into prominence as leader of the 1913 strike-lockout of transit workers in Dublin, which got so much attention in Socialist circles that Lenin wrote glowingly about Larkin as the conflict was unfolding. He was an associate of James Connolly, the Irish nationalist martyr, and in fact, Larkin was the senior partner in that relationship until he left for America. His rhetoric combined religion, Irish nationalism, and Marxism indiscriminately and without apology. His last act before he left for America symbolized that mix: he visited Liverpool, where he had been born and lived briefly, and left Socialist literature in a time capsule that he placed in the foundation of a church under construction.

Larkin's trip to America in October 1914, shortly after the conclusion of the Dublin conflict, was officially described as a fund-raising effort for his union. But he probably wanted a new and bigger stage.

He had developed a close relationship with the Socialist Party and the IWW, both of which had actively supported him in the Dublin strike. There was also an affinity of ideas; he shared the Socialist Party's vociferous opposition to World War I and the IWW's "One Big Union" syndicalist vision, which was very similar to Larkinism. He set up residence in New York but toured the country for four years, speaking under the auspices of those two organizations, a fact the prosecution brought out in his criminal anarchy trial.

Larkin came to Communism much as Bill Haywood and John Reed had — after an extensive history in left-wing politics. When he first participated in the Socialist Party debates and then in the creation of early Communism, his reputation preceded him. Gitlow's compatriot Bertram Wolfe wrote that Larkin "appeared in our midst surrounded by legend." At that point, Larkin saw Bolshevism as the best horse to ride in his lifelong crusade against economic inequality, and like many other pre-Bolshevik radicals, he saw the Soviet Union as the realization of his life's work. He was a man of action, not polemics; to him, the appeal of a Leninist party was as a means to achieve his goals. He did not enjoy or indulge in the theoretical debates that came naturally to some of the other defendants.

Larkin and Gitlow, both leaders of the Left Wing Socialists and the Communist Labor Party, were arraigned and jailed together. Gitlow was not questioned by the district attorney's office on the night of his arrest, but Larkin was, extensively. He was considered important enough that Archibald Stevenson conducted the interview. Though strong willed, Larkin was guileless and incapable of declining to answer a challenging question. Walter Nelles was with him in the police station and later wrote that Stevenson "traded upon Larkin's characteristic scorn of his constitutional privilege of silence." Nelles advised Larkin to remain silent, but that was not a right that appealed to him. In the indictment issued from the Magistrate's Court, William McAdoo referred to the "illuminating statement of the defendant Larkin" as being helpful in understanding and explaining the illegalities in *Revolutionary Age*. The "Left Wing Manifesto" "must be read in connection with the statements of Larkin," especially his statement to the district attorney that the manifesto "had several authors but one mind." In Rorke's cross-examination of Larkin during the trial, he read sections of that interview verbatim, including Larkin's insistence that the manifesto "totally" represented his sentiments and that he advocated it "absolutely."

Larkin chose to represent himself, with out-of-court help from Nelles. He had already seen two famous — and expensive — lawyers fail to keep their clients out of jail and saw no need to pay high fees for the same outcome. He also had great faith in his own ability to sway an audience. He had done a legendary job in presenting the union's side of the Dublin strike to the British Board of Inquiry, besting high-powered lawyers on the other side in the process.

The beginning of the trial had very little to do with Larkin. Rorke's opening statement was generic; he mentioned Larkin's name only five times — four times as part of the National Council of the Left Wing. For purposes of this trial, Rorke added the phrase "by word of mouth" to the charge that the defendant had urged the overthrow of the American government by writings, since Larkin was best known for his rabble-rousing speeches. Rorke also made his usual attempt to define what it meant to advocate illegal means. In fact, this was his best effort. "We are not concerned during the trial, with the question as to whether it would be better for the citizens of the United States to have the Soviet form of government here . . . [or] to have the ancient feudal system. . . . All that we are interested in here is the means, the ways they intend to bring about the change." Larkin had played a highly visible role at the Left Wing convention, so Rorke believed that all he needed to do was introduce the convention's decisions and present some speeches made by Larkin to demonstrate that he advocated illegal means.

Rorke built his case around the testimony of Joseph Zinman, a stenographer hired to make an official record of the convention. Zinman affirmed that Larkin's name appeared in his notes, that he had approved the actions of the convention, and that he had led a chant of "Three cheers for the social revolution!" Rorke also had the stenographer read into the record a lengthy speech Larkin had made to the convention about the need for a left-wing newspaper. It was typical Larkin — impassioned, moralistic, and with a fair amount of hyperbole — but by no fair standard could it be said to advocate illegal means of any kind:

In Seattle we have an illustration of what the organized power of a Proletariat can do in action when guided by men who know what the struggle really is.

We want to explain the significance of the Seattle strike and what is the meaning of that movement. That is the purpose of the Left Wing paper. . . . Do exactly as the missionaries in the religious organizations gets hold of the mind. Make them use their brains and understand where they are and what their place in society is. Then you will break down the bigotry and intolerance towards socialism and then you come along with the *Revolutionary Age*, and you give them the right foundation, the knowledge which will increase their purpose and intelligence. This paper should have no trimmings to it.

That Rorke believed this speech argued for conviction rather than acquittal demonstrates the elasticity of the bad tendency doctrine. Larkin was clearly enthusiastic about the Left Wing convention, and it produced literature that a jury might conclude would induce someone to commit an illegal act sometime. However, the closest the speech came to advocating anything illegal was a vague mention of the strike in Seattle (not Winnipeg) and some positive references to the IWW. This may be the clearest indication in all four trials that Rorke's standard — "the ways in which they intend to bring about the changes" — did not differ in any meaningful way from prohibiting speech that the government felt did not serve its purposes.

At the beginning of the trial, Weeks tried hard to accommodate Larkin in his role as counsel, and Larkin worked hard to project a lawyerly demeanor. Weeks ruled on objections even though Larkin could not put them in the proper form, and at one point he admonished Rorke not to put questions to Larkin as the defendant when he was acting in his capacity as counsel. He twice advised Larkin on the danger of admitting things into evidence too quickly, even though Larkin had not raised any objections. But the facade of cooperation degenerated as the trial went on. Larkin twice apologized for outbursts of anger at the judge; Weeks grudgingly accepted but noted that Larkin did not seem to realize that it would be better to stop the behavior that necessitated the apologies. Finally, decorum broke down completely. Larkin was cross-examining Lovatt, the Winnipeg witness, and was trying to prove that the general strike had been legally called and conducted, when Rorke raised an objection. That set Larkin off, and he lost the courtroom manner he had tried to cultivate. "I cannot prove it if the Court, and the Assistant District Attorney desire to try and obscure with meaningless interruptions the mental intercourse of thought between this defendant and the Witness." Weeks then matched him in dropping the legal veneer. "Such language, Mr. Larkin, can only be properly met . . . by the imposition of a punishment, which in view of the fact that you are a defendant on trial here, would seem very much to be sending coals to Newcastle." In essence, Weeks was saying — in front of the jury — that since Larkin would be going to jail at the end of the trial anyway, citing him for contempt would be superfluous.

The trial took its most entertaining twist when Larkin examined himself from the witness stand, asking "the defendant" questions and then answering them:

LARKIN: Did the defendant or any of his co-defendants ever advocate the use of violence?
LARKIN: No, on the contrary, always decried violence.

He used the question-response format to outline his goal of a "socialistic, industrial democracy form of government," an honest description of his unrefined vision. Then he went into the legally crucial question of the means employed to get there. He queried himself as to whether "political action" could be used to reach that end and answered that it could be, the implication being that voting was one means, but only one among several. Was it sufficient? Weeks asked the obvious follow-up: "The question is not whether the ballot shall be used, is it your contention that the result can be accomplished by the use of the ballot?" Larkin: "No."

That was Rorke's takeoff point for his cross-examination. He got Larkin to discuss what he advocated in addition to voting and constitutional change. Larkin had used the ambiguous term "direct action" and then specified (unwisely) that one form of direct action was "to take up arms to resist oppression," although he added that assassination was never included in the meaning of direct action. Rorke repeatedly tried to pin Larkin down as to the specific extraparliamentary means he advocated, implying that they had to involve violence. But

Larkin would only say that the state could be transformed by "education," by "mass psychology," and by "ideas promulgated, until all the people adopt them." Rorke, believing he had found his trump card, asked Larkin whether it had ever happened that "moral suasion caused the possessor of property to turn it over to one who has no property." Larkin was undaunted. "It was done in Judea, and the Christian Church to which I belong, which was a Communist Church for four centuries, and all things were held in common. . . . No man had the right to give or sell any portion of the national territory, had no right except in the personal adornment of his person." It was the perfect Larkin blend: idealistic, combative, Christian, Marxist, Irish.

He tried to combine those elements again in his three-and-a-half-hour summary, but this time he veered into incoherence. He spoke movingly at times — recounting, for instance, how the poverty he had seen in Liverpool as a child led to his moral outrage about economic injustice. But not much of his closing was directed toward acquittal. He tried to divorce himself from the manifesto but could not make up his mind: "I would not allow a paper like that to go out, if I were the editor. There were things in it I would not submit to, and yet for the general body of the paper, I think it is one of the most intelligent and best informed and historically accurate papers in the country." He quoted Abraham Lincoln, Woodrow Wilson, and Charles Beard. He dropped the names of Walt Whitman, Mark Twain, Henry David Thoreau, Albert Einstein, Galileo, and Wendell Phillips and invoked Valley Forge. He argued that Socialism was a religion, protected under the free exercise clause of the First Amendment, and he challenged the testimony of the Jewish stenographer on the grounds that he could not have taken his courtroom oath seriously because it had been sworn on the New Testament. At one point in the summary, Weeks interjected, "You are losing your head."

His conclusion may not have been a precise refutation of legal charges, but it was a good representation of Larkin's mind-set:

[The defendant] is getting tried for within his mind focusing the ideas of the centuries, and trying to bring knowledge into co-ordinate form that he might assist and develop and beautify life. That is the charge against the defendant — that he preached a doctrine of humanity against inhumanity; that he preached a doctrine of order against disorder; that he preached the doctrine of brotherhood as against that mischievous, hellish thing of national and brute herd hatred.

Rorke's closing was pro forma, repeating large parts of his previous closings — describing the manifesto as "an outpouring of Hell itself" and even a "Red Ruby in the Red Treasure Chest." He inserted a gratuitous slap at Larkin as a fake Irishman: "My mother and father were born in Ireland — born in Ireland — real bona fide Irish people." And he announced, as he did in other trials, that this time the real mastermind, the power behind the throne, was on trial. "This is the leader, the most sinister force in America today, this is the hand that pulled the strings." The idea that Larkin — this most public, flamboyant, emotive orator — was a secret manipulator confirms what Gitlow wrote about Rorke twenty years later — that he did not believe half of what he said. But he knew the verdict was foreordained. It was — it took the jury less than an hour to convict.

After the Gitlow and Winitsky convictions, Larkin's case broke no new legal ground. But it did recapitulate the logic of the previous trials — that agreement with and diffuse responsibility for the ideas of the manifesto constituted a violation of the criminal anarchy law, because illegal means could be inferred from its words. Nothing illustrated that better than a phrase Weeks and Rorke seized on from one of Larkin's public speeches. Rorke asked him whether he had used the phrase "the Communists must march forward with the Red flag on their bayonets." Larkin strongly denied saying that, even though a stenographer had taken it down. After the verdict, Weeks asked Larkin again if he would admit to using those words, and Larkin again denied it. Judge, prosecutor, and defendant all understood how damning that phrase was, even though it was the most obvious of metaphors. When "advocacy of illegal means" can be deduced from a statement of goals, metaphorical bayonets are as lethal as real ones.

A Matter for Open Public Discussion

If the Larkin trial involved the most internationally recognizable defendant, the finale involved two people at the very center of American Communism: Isaac E. Ferguson and Charles E. Ruthenberg. Ruthenberg was, for a time, the Comintern-appointed leader of the party. Gitlow, whose account in *I Confess* was largely hostile to Ruthenberg ("insufferably egotistical"), nonetheless admitted Ruthenberg's centrality to the divided world of American Communism. "He did become the one in whom the power of our Party seemed vested for all eternity. He was the hub around which the wheel turned." Ruthenberg went through four serious felony trials between 1918 and 1924, leading the *Chicago Tribune* to describe him as "the most arrested Red in America." The last of his four convictions was being contested in the Supreme Court when he died in 1927. Some of his remains were shipped to the Soviet Union, where he joined John Reed and Bill Haywood as the only Americans buried in or near the Kremlin Wall.

Ruthenberg's codefendant, Ferguson, served as counsel for both of them. He was a graduate of the University of Chicago Law School, where he was involved in the pre-Bolshevik Socialist movement. Then he spent four years in Wyoming, where he ran for county attorney as a Republican. Ferguson moved back to Chicago in 1918 and reentered the leftist politics he had dabbled in at law school. What was unusual about Ferguson was his rapid and complete movement back and forth between his two identities—Communist and lawyer. When speaking or writing as a Communist, he sounded very much like every other leading figure. But when he spoke as a lawyer, he was polished, non-confrontational, deferential to judicial norms, and very precise in his arguments—as though he had gone into a phone booth and changed into a mild-mannered reporter. He had helped write the defense brief in Eugene Debs's Supreme Court case and had worked on the brief in Rose Pastor Stokes's successful appeal.

The prosecutor's case was built on the same formula that had already produced three convictions: stenographers testified about speeches Ferguson and Ruthenberg had made at the Left Wing convention, office workers testified that they had interacted with the defendants in New York, and the printer of *Revolutionary Age* established a chain of ownership that went up to the National Council of the Left Wing Socialists. George Robert Lovatt gave 130 pages of Winnipeg testimony, finally getting into the record the words written on the red cards distributed to businesses that were allowed to stay open ("Permitted by authority of the Strike Committee"). Although this trial was most notable for Ruthenberg's exposition on the basics of Communism from the witness stand, Ferguson's defense should not be overlooked. Winning an acquittal was not likely, so he concentrated on laying the groundwork for an appeal.

One appeal issue was the constitutionality of the criminal anarchy law. Each previous defense counsel had touched on it, none successfully. Ferguson made it more central in his presentation. He moved for dismissal at the outset, on the grounds that "the facts in the indictment do not constitute a crime" and that "any conviction would be null and void as in derogation of the liberties" guaranteed by the New York and U.S. constitutions. Then he invoked Oliver Wendell Holmes's "clear and present danger" test, offered less than two years earlier in *Schenck v. United States*. From that case, Ferguson concluded that for advocacy of illegal activity to be prohibited, it must be aimed at someone specific who might carry it out. The case against Ruthenberg and himself did not fit. "There is nothing chargeable as an advocacy which is not directed to some set of hearers, and . . . it must be a set of hearers who can do something about it." Weeks recognized the argument and noted, "You have in mind the language of the Mr. Justice Holmes. . . . But this indictment is not under the Espionage Act." Ferguson responded, "But the principle is the same, if it is an indictment founded upon advocacy, I assume we are not charged with emitting certain sounds. We are charged with getting over certain ideas to certain people." Weeks rejected the motion to dismiss with no further comment.

In his closing, Ferguson compared the criminal anarchy law with the Sedition Act of 1798 and pointed to the popular rejection of that act and the Jefferson administration's restitution of the fines paid by those convicted under it. Weeks interrupted to complain that Ferguson was arguing for jury nullification. In reality, he had been, but he denied it and abruptly shifted his speech rights argument to the overbroad interpretation of the law. "It is the easiest thing in the world to take any political propaganda to which you are opposed, and figure out how it is force and violence propaganda, the easiest thing in the world."

The other part of Ferguson's defense strategy was more prosaic, but also more likely to pay off at some level of appeal. He tried to put as much time and distance as possible between the two defendants and the "Left Wing Manifesto." Ferguson and Ruthenberg admitted their national leadership role in the Left Wing Socialists – they could hardly deny it – but claimed an almost total lack of knowledge about the manifesto. This was not a strategy available to Gitlow, as *Revolutionary Age*'s business manager, or to Winitsky, a hands-on local party leader who had helped set up its distribution. It might have been available to Larkin if he had hired a lawyer rather than representing himself. The issue of the defendants' responsibility for the manifesto came early in Rorke's opening statement when he mentioned Gitlow's name. Ferguson objected to the reference, asking what relevance the activities of "a man named Gitlow" had. Weeks responded, as he often did, by explaining the prosecution's case: "Now there must be a connection to the defendants here. The District Attorney claims the connection is shown by the election of the defendant Gitlow as business manager of this paper, which paper was being conducted by the National Council, of which these defendants on trial were members."

Ferguson countered, "By being members of the National Council the defendants should take on whatever responsibility might arise out of articles of Mr. Gitlow as business manager of that paper?" Ferguson tried to demonstrate a flaw in that logic in several ways. First, he asked almost every prosecution witness whether they had had any contact with Ruthenberg or himself with regard to the "Left Wing Manifesto." Predictably, the answer was always no. He also asked in his closing argument why the State had chosen to prosecute for the manifesto rather than for the Left Wing's program, which the defendants admitted writing. "Why? Oh, because forsooth, they think there are a few phrases in the Manifesto which are rather murky and look like they might mean something that might be seen to have something to do with the Criminal Anarchy law of New York."

The certainty of a conviction meant that, in addition to laying the basis for an appeal, there was little to stop Ferguson and Ruthenberg from using the trial as a forum for advertising their political views. The highlight was Ruthenberg's testimony, a rollicking, virtually unconstrained exchange about the basic precepts of Marxism and Bolshevism. Ruthenberg took a more orthodox approach to Marxism than either Gitlow or Larkin and made no concessions at all to try to make his views more palatable. Weeks may have seen this as his best chance to do what he loved, which was to engage Marxist theorists and demonstrate that their own logic led to illegalities. He also may have seen the unapologetic Ruthenberg as a worthy adversary; certainly, the discussion was conducted with a measure of surface respect.

Ferguson's role in direct examination was simply to feed Ruthenberg questions. The recital began with an explanation of the Left Wing's differences with the Socialist Party. "The Party should assume the position of demanding merely one thing, and that is the abolition of the capitalist system," said Ruthenberg. "Also that the Socialist Party . . . had become more or less a vote getting machine to elect certain persons to public offices, rather than an organization which sought to bring about a fundamental change in the social system." When Ferguson tried to move on to other topics, Weeks actually stopped him and encouraged Ruthenberg to explain himself more fully. That began a direct exchange between Weeks and Ruthenberg:

> WEEKS: You used an unusual word there, "expropriate." . . . What is the meaning of the word as you use it?
> RUTHENBERG: The taking by the state, the existing government of certain properties necessary for the whole of societies. . . .
> WEEKS: Does that include any proposals for the workers as groups, or as individuals, taking property, taking industries from capitalist owners?
> RUTHENBERG: The only proposal is that the state or government shall take the property.

Weeks and Ruthenberg then discussed whether the expropriation would be compensated, whether the former owners would be allowed to vote, and what the dictatorship of the proletariat meant. At the end of direct examination, Ferguson gave Ruthenberg a chance to explain what "revolutionary class struggle" meant. He refused to soften its implications: "not a struggle merely for better wages and working conditions, but to change the relation between the wage worker and capitalist and abolish the capitalist ownership of industry."

Rorke started his cross-examination by exploring the familiar question of whether Ruthenberg advocated illegal means, but Weeks quickly commandeered the questioning. "Is there a transition period between capitalism and socialism?" he asked. "Now a proletarian state involves something in the nature of a form of government?" Rorke became a spectator during what should have been his own cross-examination, at one point objecting in frustration to an answer Ruthenberg gave to a question by Weeks. On redirect examination by Ferguson, there was no attention at all to judicial procedure — it resembled a three-way bull session among Weeks, Ruthenberg, and Ferguson. Weeks asked a long question about how Ruthenberg would deal with different rates of saving among wage earners, and Ruthenberg responded by blaming capitalism for "constant friction and constant struggle," whereupon Weeks asked what effect the expropriation of savings would have on ambition and initiative. Courtroom norms began to lapse into burlesque. When Weeks (not Ferguson) asked Ruthenberg about rates of pay in Russia, Ferguson (not Ruthenberg) responded by asking the judge whether he had read a book entitled *Bolshevism at Work*. Weeks wanted to know when it had been published and whether it reflected recent changes. And when Weeks sardonically asked Ruthenberg for a copy of the constitution of the Soviet Union ("I gave mine away yesterday"), Ferguson walked to the bench and handed him one. The absurdity of the spectacle finally became too much for Rorke, who objected that he had serious work to do. "Your Honor, I want to interpose an objection to continuing this line of examination further. I apprehend, sir, that I have three things to attempt to establish in this case, one there is an organized government here. . . . " But Weeks was having too much fun and cut him off in mid objection, saying, "Do not discuss it." Just before Ruthenberg left the stand, Weeks stumped him twice. First he asked what, in Ruthenberg's scenario, would happen to the president, "who has taken an oath of office to carry on this government under the Constitution." Ruthenberg responded, "I am unable to say what would become of [him]." Then Weeks wanted to know what would happen to the gold in the subtreasury. Ruthenberg responded, "The Court's view of that is as good as mine. I do not know anything about that." This was not a debater's point for Weeks; he was trying to demonstrate why the creation of the new revolutionary order Ruthenberg proposed would, by its very nature, involve large-scale violations of legal order and property rights.

Rorke need not have worried about proving his case. The likely reason the three principals felt unconstrained by legal convention was that there was nothing at stake. The jury found Ferguson and Ruthenberg guilty in less than two hours. Nor did the exchange of ideas, in spite of the friendly, conversational tone, lessen the antagonism between the judge and the defendants. When Weeks asked each of them to state why he should not impose the maximum penalty, Ruthenberg made a short, forceful statement of defiance, "accepting this [the verdict] as a case of the use of the organized force of the state in order to suppress the desires of those who today are suffering under the oppression of the present system." Ferguson said that Weeks had "acted as prosecutor in this case from beginning to end." Weeks lectured Ferguson that although he did not expect Ruthenberg to understand judicial process, Ferguson was a lawyer and should know better. Then he imposed the same penalties as in the other three cases.

The four cases had been mini-dramas involving defiant and prickly personalities on both sides, varying defense strategies, and intense arguments about Marxist principles, tempered by the knowledge that, after the *Gitlow* verdict, there was no mystery about the outcome. One of the goals of the defendants had been to proselytize — jury, public, and future generations. But another goal of the defense lawyers had been to suggest a more coherent and expanded approach to speech rights, even for those who — like these defendants — described themselves as revolutionaries. Darrow suggested that Gitlow was a harmless dreamer. Larkin argued that his views were a modern-day version of the Sermon on the Mount. Fallon argued more carefully that Winitsky had not incited anyone to do anything other than to read party material. At the end of his closing statement, Ferguson the civil libertarian lawyer again elbowed out Ferguson the Communist, placing speech rights in the context of democratic dialogue:

> I do not ask you by your verdict to say we are right. . . . What we do ask is that you shall say whatever is the truth or falsity of these doctrines, it is a matter for open public discussion.
>
> If we are wrong, let us be answered. If we are right, is this the way to fight us?

———

Postmortems

Gust Alonen and Carl Paivio did not appeal their convictions, mainly due to a lack of funds. They served three and a half years of their four-year sentences and were released. They became Communists in prison, partly through contact with Gitlow, Larkin, and Winitsky. Paivio remained a lifelong Communist; at the time of his death in 1952, he was facing deportation proceedings for his political activities.

The Communist defendants appealed, and the appellate court upheld all their convictions, without a dissenting vote. Gitlow's case, which by now had been selected by the Civil Liberties Bureau as its test case, was argued first and produced the only substantial opinion, which is discussed in the next chapter. Larkin's new lawyer argued that the other defendants were ideologues and that his client "was devoted to a different kind of propaganda than the other men in the left wing." Ferguson wrote Winitsky's appeal, arguing that a conviction based on inferences from publications opened the door for widely expanded governmental suppression of speech rights: "Yet under this statute, at any point of time, any member must answer an accusation of felony for the exact details of party declarations. . . . No matter that decades and even centuries of changes in the doctrines themselves may intervene before the time of fulfillment in action. Here is a doctrine which opens up possibilities never before dreamt of in American criminal law."

The appellate court rejected both Larkin's and Winitsky's appeals without comment, although the justices had made their position on the former clear enough during oral arguments: "Is Larkin responsible for the manifesto or not? That's all we want to know. It doesn't matter what kind of man he is. It doesn't matter if he is the head of a church." Both men dropped their appeals after the appellate court hearing.

The Ferguson-Ruthenberg appeal was based on the issue of their responsibility for the "Left Wing Manifesto." First, the judges in the Appellate Division ruled that since the defendants were on the National Council of the Left Wing and had not immediately disavowed the article, they should be held liable for it. It was later, at the court of appeals, that Ferguson's careful trial work to distance the two of them from the manifesto paid off. The appeals court ruled six to one that legal responsibility had not been proved, pointing out, for instance, that both defendants had returned to the Midwest two weeks before the manifesto was published and before there was agreement on what it should contain. The court ordered them released, pending a new trial, but it was never held. Ruthenberg was immediately confronted with his next set of charges, which eventually resulted in the Supreme Court case *Ruthenberg v. Michigan*. Ferguson quietly dropped out of leftist politics shortly after his conviction was reversed, although he did represent his friend Ruthenberg in the Supreme Court case. In 1928 he also argued for a Communist alien who was being deported. After that, although he continued to practice law and argued in the Supreme Court four times, there is no record of his involvement in any cases dealing with leftists or civil liberties. Ferguson's final Supreme Court argument was in 1963, representing California avocado growers who were trying to keep Florida avocados out of their market. He won.

On January 17, 1923, Governor Al Smith pardoned Larkin. After briefly disassociating himself from any of Larkin's views, he explained his decision:

> There is no evidence that Larkin ever endeavored to incite any specific acts of violence or lawlessness. . . . Political progress results from the clash of conflicting opinions. The public assertion of an erroneous doctrine is perhaps the surest way to disclose the error. . . . And it is a distinct disservice of the State to impose, for the utterances of a misguided opinion, such extreme punishment as may tend to deter that full and free discussion of political issues which is a fundamental of democracy.

Larkin stayed in the country four more months, raising money for a proposed food ship to Ireland. When the shipment did not materialize he went to Washington, according to a biographer, "for the sole purpose of forcing the government to deport him." On April 20 he was put on a ship and headed home. There is a statue of Larkin in Dublin, with these words by playwright Sean O'Casey on its base: "He talked to the workers, spoke only as Jim Larkin could speak . . . trumpet-tongued of resistance to wrong, discontent with leering poverty, and defiant of any power strutting out to stand in the way of their march forward."

Winitsky was pardoned a year after Larkin. His appeal had been the last one rejected in the appellate court, and Smith pardoned him a month later. The pardon statement was brief: "I am satisfied that Winitsky has been sufficiently punished for the crime which he has committed and I have accordingly granted him a pardon." A news account described his reaction:

> Winitsky is celebrating by turning the tables on the world. At a ball given here by the National Defence Council, there will be a good-natured farce, in which Winitsky will play the role of judge. Ben Gitlow [out on bail], a former cell mate of Winitsky at Dannemora State Prison, will be the sargeant of police. Winitsky will spend the evening sentencing his comrades to 20 and 30 cent fines for dancing with another man's wife — or their own — proceeds to be devoted to the political prisoners' fund.

Gitlow in Jail, *Gitlow* in Court

When Gitlow was first sentenced, his Bolshevik resolve momentarily wavered. "The realization that I was no longer a free man struck home. . . . When I was locked up in my cell, I was in a daze. I rose and paced up and down like a wild beast in a cage. The walls of the cell seemed to move about me in confusing circles." He quickly regained his composure. His explanation of how he did so is, in some ways, the most interesting part of his autobiography. The story is not one of self-congratulatory martyrdom but one of a strong and resourceful person determined to face adversity and overcome it. "I am not the only one who has ever gone to prison. Many have gone, some for a much longer time. . . . If they were able to survive, why can't I?"

His total time in prison was close to three years, longer than any of the others convicted with him. He served from February 13, 1920, to April 25, 1922; then, beginning on September 7, he served three more months following an unfavorable court of appeals verdict. He was moved from Sing Sing to Clinton Prison in upstate New York and then to Auburn Prison, returning every so often to Sing Sing. In a review of *I Confess*, political psychologist Harold Laswell called Gitlow's account of his time in prison that of "a matter-of-fact observer and writer singularly untouched by sentimentalism." There is no parallel in Gitlow's voluminous writings and speeches to the prison chapter in *I Confess*. Whereas his other accounts tend to lack subtlety, his prison writing does not. It is warm, humorous, and complex—the last a quality almost completely absent elsewhere in his two books.

In the earliest of many letters written to her son in prison, Kate Gitlow noted, "It is a comfort that you are taking things philosophically." That was the touchstone of Gitlow's outlook on his prison experience, and he counseled his parents to adopt it: "Nothing would please me more than to know that you are not fretful or weeping over my confinement here but to know that you are taking the matter philosophically." Before his own trial, Isaac E. Ferguson visited all the criminal anarchy prisoners and wrote his observations in a party newspaper. He found that Winitsky and especially the hyperactive Larkin were having trouble adjusting to confinement. But "Alonen and Gitlow are men of self-contained type who are to a considerable extent able to live within themselves. They succeed in making a pretty good best out of a bad situation."

Gitlow quickly and easily learned how the informal prison networks worked — how to get meals and clothes and how to send letters without their being read — and adapted to them. He struck up a friendship with a Catholic chaplain, even after admitting that he was Jewish by background and an atheist by belief. In his first meeting with Gitlow, the chaplain delicately inquired whether Gitlow might want "certain books which we do not have in our library." He agreed to see that Gitlow got those books, "provided . . . you will not pass them around to the other inmates in the system." Gitlow knew how to play the game: "I gave him that promise. Did I keep it? Of course not! I am sure he never expected me to, but just put it that way in order to protect himself if anything happened." He wrote with a similar air of bemusement when he encountered things that bothered him. He mentioned his instinctual revulsion at the homosexual practices in prison but recorded what he saw without excessive moralizing: "Why this colored man was called a man I do not know. Not only was he feminine in all his action and characteristics, but in him they were exaggerated. I never saw a person in prison more jolly than he."

He took note of inmates who were crazy or violent, wardens who were mean and vindictive, and doctors who were manipulative, but he chronicled them as if they were playing roles in a comedy. They never seemed to bother him much personally or to intrude on his "philosophical" calm. When he was moved from Sing Sing to Clinton, he wrote to a friend, "Prisons are no longer cruel mysteries to me. I have come to know them quite well." If there were no contemporaneous prison letters, it would be tempting to attribute the reflections on prison life in his 1939 autobiography to the healing power of time and his friendlier attitude toward American justice than in his Communist period. But there is nothing in the prison chapter of *I Confess* that is at odds with the two dozen letters to and from Gitlow during his confinement.

What is notably absent from his description of prison is any indictment of the penal system as an example of the injustice of the capitalist system. Larkin constantly railed against the humiliating conditions in prison, and as Ferguson noted, it made him miserable. "Larkin is dominated by a fierce sense of social justice. He meets continually with things that burn him. . . . This quality of his causes him more suffering in prison than insults or bad physical conditions." Gitlow noted conditions that he could have used to rage against capitalist dungeons — worms in the cereal, a procedure for emptying excrement buckets that guaranteed getting splashed — but he simply recounted how he dealt with them. Gitlow had been sentenced to "hard labor," which he described as moving a few bricks a day: "When the newspapers reported I was sweating on a rockpile, I was . . . sitting around in Yard Two listening to the stories of woe of my fellow convicts." He also noted in his letters and in *I Confess* the positive features of each of the prisons — liberal reforms at Sing Sing, and Clinton's location in "one of nature's prettiest and healthiest spots."

He seemed to be uninterested in imposing the language of class oppression and class struggle onto prison conditions. Only when he discussed what brought people to prison did his political views surface, but they were less Marxist than "root cause" liberal humanism. Inmates were miscreants with hearts of gold — good people driven to bad deeds by their backgrounds. The prisoner he described most sympathetically was a poor, violent, young Irish American man from New York City he called "Angel Face":

I liked him, although he was known as a killer. . . . [B]eneath this veneer was a youth with a heart that could feel genuinely and deeply with sympathy for the underdog, a sense of justice, and a willingness to fight for what he thought was right. . . . [F]undamentally, he was a sound young man in rebellion against the social abnormalities of his environment that crippled his youth. . . . What appealed to me most in him was his innate defiance of life as it is. In that, surely he was a revolutionist in temper, truly my comrade.

This romanticism represents the only indictment of the overall system in Gitlow's prison observations, and even here, he is not railing against the institutions of the penal system or against anything done specifically to him. His social critique is exclusively about what drives people to become criminals, and his views are more Tom Joad than Lenin. "Every lawbreaker whose life has been spent in poverty and in the slums believes that society owes him something. Lawbreakers of this type are individualists, seeking in their individual way, as lawbreakers, to solve their problems. Legal authority makes no attempt to understand the victim."

His lighthearted observations about the rigors of confinement should not obscure the fact that Gitlow's Communist commitment was hardening during his jail time. When his friend and political ally John Reed died, Gitlow sent a passionate message to be read at a party funeral: "When the working class, free from bondage, will take up the task of reconstructing society on a communist basis, John Reed will be honored by the revolutionary hosts as one of the many heroes who gave their lives for the revolution."

In 1921, while in prison, Gitlow ran for mayor of New York, and Winitsky ran for president of the Board of Aldermen. Gitlow's status on the ballot was the subject of another court action. He was first ruled ineligible by the Board of Elections, then ruled eligible on appeal ("in the present state of the law, our courts seem powerless to prevent such an outrage on decency"); finally, he was taken off the ballot, definitively, by the Appellate Division ("The Court will not lend its aid to the accomplishment of an absurd and foolish thing"). Even so, Gitlow wrote a "campaign speech" that veered more toward Communist orthodoxy than had his trial speech two years earlier. The "workers' control of industry" language was gone, replaced by an unambiguous call to overthrow capitalism and its government. All the criminal anarchy defendants had tried to create enough space between government and industry to confuse the issue of what it was they were advocating overthrowing; Gitlow now collapsed that space. "The working class and the capitalist class are facing each other as opposing armies in deadly combat. . . . The government of the United States is a class government. The destruction of capitalism at all times is the issue confronting the working class. . . . Abolish capitalism and its bloody political tyrannical rule." Even that was not quite enough for the Gitlow of 1921; his handwritten version of the speech sent from prison added: "But a working class government can only be gained as a result of a revolution on the part of the working class."

Revolution also dominated Gitlow's letters to and from his parents. But in this case, it was not so much what he wrote as what he received. He warned his parents that he could say very little about national or party affairs in his letters, for fear it would get him in trouble with prison authorities. His mother, his alter ego in the world of Communism in those years, had no reason to be circumspect, and her letters came alive when she brought tidings of revolution to him: "The sun is rising and the New Year is beginning with bigger hope for our ideals." Sometimes she passed along messages: "I have for you hearty greetings from Big Bill H. [Haywood]." And sometimes she wrote about his case: "When I see the big flow of people interested in you, I feel that everything will be done to get justice for you." At other times she sent her thoughts on news, such as the death of John Reed: "Ben, you know better than I do that the great ideals for which Jack fought require great sacrifice." She reflected on the anniversary of Rosa Luxemburg's death: "She was a great woman. In our memory is impressed those great historical days in which she and comrade K. L. [Karl Liebknecht] stood out like two shining angels." Most of all, she wrote about Ben being freed and assuming the mantle of leadership in the revolutionary ranks that prison had earned him: "I see the truth marching on. I know that my son is a great and kind man, who loves mankind. I can see surely that it is not far away and the people will understand you."

————

Exit Strategies

During the time Gitlow was in prison, one by one those who had been tried with him were released by either court decision or pardon. He could serve time with equanimity as part of his revolutionary commitment, but he was distinctly unhappy about some of the decisions his associates had made. He disapproved of Lovestone's testimony in the Winitsky trial, believing (wrongly) that it played a crucial role in the verdict. He knew that Ferguson and Ruthenberg had argued that, as Communist leaders but not newspaper editors, they bore no legal responsibility for *Revolutionary Age* and that Gitlow, as business manager, had made all the decisions about articles for the paper and had not informed them. Gitlow's conduct at his own trial was (and always remained) a source of pride for him, and he believed that Ferguson and Ruthenberg had failed to display revolutionary fortitude in distancing themselves from the newspaper. It bothered him even more that they had tried to put responsibility for the manifesto entirely on him. In a draft of *I Confess*, he wrote, then crossed out, this comment on Ferguson's "blame Gitlow first" strategy: "I did not believe my eyes when I read of the line of argument he followed." From a practical perspective, it made good sense for a Communist defendant to put the whole burden on someone who was already in jail and could not be further punished. But Gitlow believed his own trial behavior had been principled and that Ferguson and Ruthenberg's blame-shifting was dishonorable. He commented acidly in a letter to his family: "I. E. [Ferguson] made a masterful defense. Too bad my shoulders weren't broad enough to permit the distinguished legal experts to leap to actual freedom." In a later appeal, Ferguson and Ruthenberg did leap to actual freedom based in large part on their plea of ignorance of the content of the manifesto, and in *I Confess*, Gitlow recounted his reaction: "I had every personal reason for detesting Ruthenberg because of his shabby action against me in the past. When we were in Sing Sing, he and Ferguson won their case on appeal by charging me with sole responsibility for the publication of *The Revolutionary Age* and the articles it contained, alleging that I, as its business manager, had taken the copy to the printer." But devotion to cause outweighed distaste for what he took to be their lack of revolutionary integrity: "In what I considered to be in the best interests of the movement, I put aside my personal feelings."

That same ability to put cause above self-interest explains Gitlow's willingness to permit his case to be taken to the Supreme Court, which required postponing an almost certain pardon. Several things are clear about the decision to make Gitlow's case the test of peacetime sedition laws. First, it was the newly formed American Civil Liberties Union (ACLU) that urged Gitlow to appeal, not vice versa. Walter Pollak, who argued the case in the Supreme Court, wrote in 1925, "We [the ACLU], who were anxious for a decision on these laws by the highest court, persuaded Gitlow to make the appeal." Second, the decision to take this case to the Supreme Court was made around the time Governor Al Smith was deciding on pardons for the convicted defendants, not before or even right after Gitlow's trial. State senator John Hastings initially submitted applications for pardons for both Winitsky and Gitlow in January 1923 (immediately after the Larkin pardon). But Smith had made it clear that "he would not consider application for pardon in cases where appeals were pending." So if Gitlow wanted to be pardoned, he and the ACLU would have to drop the appeal. Instead, Pollak convinced Hastings to withdraw his pardon application for Gitlow. "We do not want the Governor to act on his case at this time, because it is important to get a decision from the Supreme Court on the constitutional issues involved." He also convinced an understandably hesitant Gitlow to go along: "Gitlow, who would prefer personally to withdraw his appeal and take a pardon, is willing to subordinate his own personal interests to the larger issue involved." Gitlow confirmed that the initiative came from the ACLU: "I had given the civil liberties union my promise, when the pardons were first issued, to waive the pardon in order to make the test."

For the ACLU, at issue in this test case was the possible expansion of protection for dissent in peacetime, after the drubbing the First Amendment had taken during the war. Since this case was based on a New York law, civil libertarians also saw an opportunity to argue that the Bill of Rights should be extended to apply to the states — the "incorporation" doctrine that became the most tangible legacy of *Gitlow*.

But why would a thoroughly committed Communist like Gitlow agree to postpone his freedom in an effort to expand what he believed to be the illusory rights of bourgeois democracy? He did not address that question explicitly. But in its early history, the ACLU was closely interwoven with leftist politics — its founder, Roger Baldwin, had gone to prison for opposing the war — and there may have been a presumed commonality of goals between the ACLU and the Communists. Also, the Communists would be the main beneficiaries of a successful challenge to state sedition laws. The Palmer raids had targeted alien leftists, making use of the government's greater latitude in immigration laws. But the criminal anarchy laws would have permitted the conviction of almost anyone who joined a Communist organization, making mere membership a crime. So the besieged Communists had a substantial self-interest in trying to get those laws overturned, despite the inconsistency of insisting that "rights" were meaningless, on the one hand, and trying to expand them, on the other. Shortly after the decision was made to appeal Gitlow's case to the Supreme Court, the National Defense Committee for Class War Prisoners issued a leaflet, asking for funds. It explained the rationale of the appeal: "Should the Court hand down a favorable decision, this case will serve as a precedent to thirty four other states where similar criminal anarchy and criminal syndicalist laws now exist. For this reason alone, the Gitlow case is of vital interest to all organizations and individuals who are interested in labor's fight." For that tangible benefit, attacks on bourgeois democracy could take a short vacation.

Pardon and appeal were only the most orthodox choices Gitlow had for leaving jail. There were more colorful alternatives. One was to jump bail and abscond to the Soviet Union, which, he claimed, several leading party figures advised him to do. They argued that Gitlow, like Ruthenberg, would face a series of never-ending charges, and rather than sit in jail for fifteen years, he could best serve Socialism by becoming a prominent political exile. Big Bill Haywood had been persuaded by Comintern officials to jump bail for exile in the Soviet Union just a year earlier, leaving those who had posted his bail in the lurch. Gitlow rejected the suggestion, largely because it seemed to be such an irrevocable commitment. He also recounted that Ruthenberg had actually planned a jailbreak, but that Ferguson had talked him out of it. The existence of that plan cannot be confirmed, but the reality of another scheme to have Gitlow avoid serving a long prison sentence seems incontrovertible. The Soviet government had offered to trade an American spy for either Gitlow or Larkin. The alleged spy was Captain Emmett Kirkpatrick, director of the Crimean division of the American Red Cross. Kirkpatrick, who was also working with American military forces allied with anti-Bolshevik Russian troops, had been captured by the Red Army in late 1920. A Soviet news agency reported preliminary talks about such an exchange. The trade never materialized, and Kirkpatrick was released in August 1921. It seems fairly clear that an exchange of some kind was discussed, although party leaders may have exaggerated its likelihood to Gitlow. With all these intrigues having come to nothing, he was left to wait out the appeals process.

No Need for Etymology

There was no unified approach to Gitlow's appeals. There were different lawyers involved, with varying political views and legal strategies. The nature of the first appeal suggests that it was not originally designated a test case and that the decision to take it to the Supreme Court was not made until 1923. *Abrams v. New York* — concerning leftists arrested for distributing a leaflet opposing America's intervention on the side of anti-Bolshevik forces — had moved directly from the trial level to the Supreme Court in 1920. By contrast, Gitlow's appeals moved through every level of state court, and the early steps were intended not to lay the basis for a constitutional fight but to get the conviction overturned by whatever approach looked most promising.

The first argument took place over a petition for a certificate of reasonable doubt, filed March 26. This certificate would permit Gitlow to be released on bond. Just as important, it would be the first test of the case's arguments in front of a judge other than Bartow Weeks. Charles Recht filed the petition, and the focus of his claim for reasonable doubt was that the New York law was unconstitutional. But to write the brief itself, Gitlow hired Charles Whitman, recent Republican governor of New York. The decision to hire Whitman caused some consternation within the party, both because Whitman was not a leftist and because he was expensive. Ferguson responded to the hiring with a memo to leadership units that all future decisions about representation would go through him. Whitman had some support among Progressives for his investigation into the Triangle Shirtwaist fire, but it was his respectability, not his slight lean to the left, that led to his hiring. Having such a mainstream figure argue the case was a kind of China-goes-to-Nixon strategy. Whitman avoided raising any broad civil liberties issues. His brief focused on the one angle he thought had the best chance of succeeding — that Gitlow had been prosecuted under a law designed for anarchists, not Communists. All but eight pages of his forty-page brief were an elaboration of that argument. The New York legislature had singled out the doctrine of anarchism as a threat to public peace; anarchists wanted to destroy existing government and leave nothing organized in its place. In contrast, Communists wanted to replace one existing government with another, the dictatorship of the proletariat, which in Soviet practice meant the centralization of authority in the state—in many ways, the antithesis of anarchism. "The Left Wing Manifesto may be seditious, it may constitute a form of crime of which the law takes, or should take, cognizance, but it is not anarchism."

This was Whitman's main selling point: Gitlow's views might be every bit as dangerous as those of anarchists, but that did not entitle the state to prosecute him under an inapplicable law. "The obvious remedy is by additional appropriate legislation." The only other issue he raised was the Winnipeg testimony—objecting to it not on the grounds that it should have been excluded by its nature but because the state's witness had no official capacity in the strike and thus almost no firsthand knowledge.

The state's case, written by district attorney Edward Swann, consisted mainly of quotes from the "Left Wing Manifesto." The implication of piling one passage of revolutionary phraseology on top of another for thirteen pages was that the defendant's misdeeds were so obvious that the defense's legal fine points were mere nitpicking. Rorke had dealt with the issue Whitman was raising by arguing at trial that Communists were closet anarchists who would not admit that their ultimate plan was an end to organized government. Swann, in the briefest of passes at addressing the issue, abandoned that unlikely argument. It was the means the Communists were advocating that violated the criminal anarchy law, he wrote, and whether their ends were the same as those of anarchists had no bearing. "If he advocated the propriety of overthrowing an existing governmental organization . . . he comes within the statute no matter what kind of government he intended should be set up in place of that to be overthrown."

Swann also touched on the issue of speech rights, even though Whitman made no mention of it, summarizing the Supreme Court's position on the World War I cases this way: "The Constitution places no restriction on the power of the legislature to punish writings or speeches which are injurious to society." He dismissed the argument against the Winnipeg testimony in half a page: "for the purposes of showing what was in fact advocated by the manifesto, it was competent for the People to show what in fact had been done." There was no overarching conclusion to Swann's brief, and he left the impression that the facts spoke for themselves.

{ *Chapter 5* }

To ruling judge John McAvoy, they did. His decision followed Swann's brief closely and admitted no room for any doubt at all, much less reasonable doubt. He responded to Whitman's distinction between anarchists and Communists with derision: although "dictionaries and encyclopedias" might define anarchism one way, the New York legislature had provided its own definition in writing the statute, and there was "no necessity of resort to purely etymological construction." There was "no reasonable doubt" that the "Left Wing Manifesto" fell within the statute's definition. Further, the Winnipeg testimony was admissible because "it is illustrative of the conditions which the advocated general strike and revolutionary mass action will bring about," and Montague's eyewitness account was as good as anyone else's in describing those conditions. Although Gitlow might not have known the details of what happened in Winnipeg when he published the article – a defense twist offered by Whitman – he should have. Ignorance is not a defense against inference. Like Swann, McAvoy rejected a First Amendment claim, even though it had not been raised. Gitlow had no right "to destroy the reputation of the citizen, the peace of society, or the existence of government." His conclusion matched Swann's: "the result was almost imperative upon the evidence presented."

The decision to use Whitman as counsel had been a rare concession to self-interest on Gitlow's part. He must have been convinced that the Republican ex-governor could argue him out of jail. Kate Gitlow wrote three letters to her son around the time of the hearing, fully anticipating that he would soon be free. On the eve of the hearing she wrote, " We expect you to be home very soon." The denial of the petition for a certificate of reasonable doubt ended the strategy of going respectable; from then on, Gitlow's appeals were handled by the left-leaning and civil libertarian lawyers Nelles, Recht, Hale, and Pollak.

————

No Specifics Necessary

The purpose of the reasonable-doubt hearing had simply been to determine whether Gitlow was eligible for bail. The first step on the path to contesting the decision itself was the Appellate Division. Hale presented the oral argument, and Recht wrote the brief. Their central issue — Recht's brief called it "the main contention" — was that the criminal anarchy law was unconstitutional. Although the brief raised other issues, including the anarchist/Communist problem and the Winnipeg testimony, it did so mainly to fortify its central argument by emphasizing that the prosecution had presented the defendant's doctrine in as lurid a light as possible to ensure conviction. The intensity and weight of the brief went into its attack on the constitutionality of naming and prohibiting a doctrine. This brief was the first extended, serious defense argument involving speech rights in the case. Recht said next to nothing about the "Left Wing Manifesto" itself, his argument being that *any* prosecution under the criminal anarchy law was constitutionally unsound. This was his core argument: "The mere spreading of any doctrine as a doctrine cannot constitutionally be declared a crime. Speaking or writing can be dealt with as a crime only when in such close relation to substantive evil condemned as criminal as to constitute an active, immediate factor toward the prohibited end."

More specifically, Recht argued that the criminal anarchy law was in violation of section 8, article 1 of the New York State Constitution ("Every citizen may freely speak, write, and publish his sentiments on all subjects, being responsible for the abuse of that right") and the due process clause of the Fourteenth Amendment to the U.S. Constitution. He made no mention of the First Amendment or of the possibility that it might prohibit state as well as federal actions. The due process clause, he claimed, "protected from invasion a still wider field of personal liberty" than the New York speech rights clause. The reason for invoking the due process clause without mentioning the First Amendment was that Recht had to thread a needle. Since the New York guarantee of speech rights explicitly permitted prosecution for abuse of those rights and the First Amendment did not, he had to smuggle the broader meaning into the more restrictive wording, and he had to do it at a time when the First Amendment was not yet thought to restrict state legislatures. But that only opened the question. According to Recht, it was "abundantly recognized and established" that the Fourteenth Amendment provided for a wide sphere of prohibitions on state legislatures, but he admitted that these rights "are not easily defined." That formulation led him where he wanted to go: suggesting a more libertarian standard for speech rights as though it were a natural extension of the due process clause.

He began in familiar territory: the Sedition Act of 1798 and its rejection by the public and the Jefferson administration (although not by the Supreme Court). Then he moved to *Reynolds v. United States* (1878), which featured (as one of its components) Mormons' right to practice polygamy. The Court had rejected that right on the grounds that the state of Utah was prohibiting a practice, not a set of religious ideas. A state could prohibit everyone equally from practicing polygamy, which is a behavior with many possible causes. But it could not stop anyone from believing in polygamy or propagating a religion that defended and promoted it. Recht concluded that *Reynolds* made a distinction between speech and action that could be applied to the *Gitlow* case. Although the practical effect of the *Reynolds* decision had been to permit the criminalization of polygamy, Recht argued that the reasoning could be inverted to find a condemnation of the bad tendency doctrine. Speech or writing that advocated illegality in the abstract could not be considered criminal merely because it might lead someone to commit illegal acts. "The practice of polygamy was held criminal," Recht argued. "It was clearly implicit, however, that belief in and advocacy of polygamy as a religious doctrine, though of unquestionably ill tendency, were immune from legislative interference." Thus, "Mormonism acceptable, polygamy not" equaled "Left Wing Manifesto acceptable, force or violence in the name of revolution not." Recht was torturing the *Reynolds* verdict slightly. Although it contained the seed of his argument, the decision probably would have been different if the beliefs at issue had not been religious ones. It took the Court fifty more years to apply the speech-action distinction to political speech.

The brief then mined recent speech-rights decisions in an effort to show that they supported that distinction. Recht admitted that an associated illegal action did not have to occur for speech to be criminal, as long as a crime was intended. But intention alone was not enough. "The act to be punished must be seen in immediate causal connection with injury, accomplished or potential." He then argued — as he had to — that the speech-rights decisions in the World War I cases had been based on a similar view. Recht made an explicit distinction between the Espionage Act of 1917 and the amendments of 1918 that made "disloyal, profane, scurrilous" language against the government, flag, or military illegal. The Espionage Act, he said, was well within constitutional boundaries because it did not make antiwar messages themselves illegal. It prohibited illegal conduct such as intending to interfere with the military, causing mutiny in the military, or obstructing recruiting. Antiwar or antidraft speech could then be judged on how close it came to inciting violations of those laws—"a question of proximity and degree," as Oliver Wendell Holmes stated in the most famous of the cases, *Schenck v. United States*. Recht did not discuss whether he thought Holmes was right in applying the law of criminal attempts to speech-rights cases. In fact, the amount of space in Recht's brief devoted to critics of Holmes's ruling—Zechariah Chaffee, Learned Hand, and Ernest Freund—makes it clear (as common sense would, also, given Recht's leftist political leanings) that he did not think the law was well applied or interpreted in those cases. But he could not criticize Holmes because his purpose and strategy were to suggest that Holmes—speaking for a unanimous Court in *Schenck*—provided the basis for the case he was making. He wanted to distinguish between a law that punished doctrine, as the criminal anarchy law did, and a law that punished conduct, as the Espionage Act did, misapplied or not.

Recht knew that his libertarian interpretation of the Espionage Act cases was a stretch. He was trying to create the impression that it was an accepted view that speech had to be in close proximity to illegal conduct to be illegal itself. If a court were to adopt his interpretation, the criminal anarchy law might be judged unconstitutional, or at the very least the *Gitlow* verdict would be overturned, since no one had ever argued that readers of the "Left Wing Manifesto" were likely to begin a general strike or an insurrection. But it was not the accepted view. Holmes had voted to uphold the *Schenck* conviction on the grounds that Socialist antiwar, antidraft messages might lead someone, somewhere, to violate the Espionage Act by evading conscription. Under the bad tendency doctrine, the illegal acts merely had to be deducible from the speech, and Recht must have known that the judges he and Hale were arguing in front of subscribed to that view.

So Recht was unlikely to get the judges to substitute his version of what was commonly accepted for their own. But there was also a logical hole in his case. His argument rested on the speech protection in the New York Constitution rather than the First Amendment, and that meant addressing the New York phrase "being responsible for the abuse of that right." Recht tried to describe what an abuse looks like and concluded that it must be speech that intends a crime and is in close proximity to the potential of a crime occurring. But that left an unanswered question — not what an abuse is, but who decides. Recht implied that the courts should. But until this case reached Oliver Wendell Holmes and Louis Brandeis on the Supreme Court, every judge explicitly ruled that the decision belonged to the New York State legislature. And that legislature had decided that words advocating that "organized government should be overthrown by force or violence" were an abuse for which the writer was responsible.

The state's brief, by John Caldwell Myers, was perfunctory, adding almost nothing to previous arguments made by the prosecution. The only interesting feature was the way it misstated and underestimated the speech-rights argument Recht was making. In a section entitled "The Real Question Involved," Myers characterized the defense argument as being that Gitlow "entertained certain political beliefs which are contrary to the beliefs entertained by the majority of our citizens — in other words, that he had been convicted of heresy." That had been Darrow's portrayal — Gitlow as a dreamer — but it was not Recht's. He did not try to convince the judges that Gitlow was a harmless eccentric. Recht's "main contention" was that the law under which Gitlow had been convicted was unconstitutional because it did not require intent and proximity. Myers did not address that. Instead, he relied on the state's trump card, which was a recital of the words of the manifesto. His opportunity came in response to the defense's contention that Rorke's summary in the trial had been less a recital of facts than a tirade. Myers more or less admitted that it was, but suggested it was no more than Gitlow deserved. "If the evidence was such as to establish the defendant's guilt of conduct which is abhorrent to patriotic men — and it *was* — the District Attorney had the right to represent such conduct in all its naked ugliness" (emphasis in original).

That language undercut the state's pious insistence that this was not a heresy case. Judge Frank Laughlin, speaking for a unanimous Appellate Division in upholding the conviction, went even further in expressing his loathing for the views at issue: "Russia is proudly pointed to as an example of proletarian dictatorship. . . . [T]he most barbaric punishment, torture, cruelty, and suffering are inflicted upon the bourgeois." That loathing at times reduced Laughlin to sputtering rage:

> If immigration is properly supervised and restricted and the people become aroused to the danger to be apprehended from the propaganda of class hatred . . . God-fearing, liberty-loving Americans both in urban and rural communities who appreciate the equal opportunities for all for bettering their status and advancement afforded by our constitutional form of government . . . will see to it that these pernicious doctrines are not permitted to take root in America.

Although Laughlin heaped abuse on Gitlow's views, he understood that Gitlow had been convicted of advocating illegal means and that certain elements were necessary to uphold the conviction. One was the finding of intent. Laughlin argued that Gitlow hoped the predicted events would take place and must have known that if they did, they would lead to violence at some point. "The defendant and his fellow-socialists of the Left Wing knew perfectly well that such results could not be peaceably accomplished." That covered intent—it was implied. Proximity? Unnecessary, because the legislature had already specified these teachings as a crime, and "the common-law theory of proximate cause . . . has no application here." If neither intent to cause illegal acts nor proximity to those acts was required, how could one find that Gitlow's conviction was not based on the inherent harmfulness of his beliefs? This was Laughlin's answer: "When people combine and advocate such doctrines, there must necessarily be great latitude for reading between the lines"—that is, "such doctrines" as Gitlow's, as opposed to others that might not be as pernicious. Scratch a bad tendency conviction, and there is a heresy conviction. It is unavoidable.

The next stop was the New York Court of Appeals. On July 22, 1922, it upheld the trial verdict, although the majority was less enthusiastic than either Laughlin or McAvoy, and there were two dissenters. Both judges who wrote for the majority implied that the sentence was excessive. Both hinted that some evidence had been improperly introduced and that Weeks had shown some prejudice against the defendant. But they concluded that the error was not substantial and did not influence the outcome. Judge Frederick Crane, writing the majority opinion, concentrated on the admissibility of the Winnipeg testimony, which he described as "not only competent, but even if incompetent, not harmful." The manifesto advocated revolution by mass strike—a new and more concise formulation of its proposed path to revolution that the state had now settled on. It offered no exact description of what a mass or general strike would look like or how it would lead to the overthrow of capitalism, but it mentioned Winnipeg as an example. Because Winnipeg had been in the news just before the manifesto was written, that would be signal enough to readers. "So notorious was the strike and suffering in Winnipeg that the court would be justified in taking judicial notice of it. . . . What the world generally knows, a court of justice may be assumed to know."

Chief Judge Frank Hiscock, in a concurrence that raised no substantive disagreements with Crane's opinion, focused on two other issues: whether the manifesto really advocated force and violence, and the anarchist/Communist problem. On the first point, he admitted that the manifesto did not directly counsel illegal acts. But "some things are so clearly incident to others that they do not need to be mentioned . . . [and] no specific words are necessary." Readers—both proponents of the manifesto and jurors in a criminal trial—would understand. And they would also understand that illegal acts would follow: "an unlawful conspiracy . . . would eventually function with force and violence."

Deducing inevitable illegality from the manifesto was in keeping with the arguments Rorke had made during the trial. But Hiscock's response to the question of whether Communists could be prosecuted as anarchists was original and creative. He found parts of the manifesto that reflected Lenin's utopian vision in *State and Revolution*: that a state was necessary only in exploitative societies and would begin to "wither away" immediately upon the overthrow of the old regime. The new "government" would not be a government at all, in the old sense; it would be the beginning of direct rule by the producers. Elements of that view showed up here and there in the manifesto ("this dictatorship is only a temporary instrument, a 'transition' state, whose task is to render states unnecessary"). Hiscock rounded up those scattered comments and concluded that the manifesto did *not* advocate replacing one government with another, since the new government, in the manifesto's own words, "is no longer a government in the old sense." Whereas the Appellate Division's decision simply held that anyone advocating political change by illegal means fell within the criminal anarchy law, Hiscock turned some of the utopian features of the Communist program against itself and presented it as advocating an end to government.

The chief judge probably took such pains on this issue because he knew that two judges were going to dissent on the grounds that the law was inapplicable to Communists. Cuthbert Pound, joined by Benjamin Cardozo, argued that there should be a new trial on more appropriate charges. Rather than pre-October Lenin, they drew on postrevolution Bolshevism to determine whether Gitlow favored a form of organized government to replace the existing one. They concluded that the manifesto urged "an organized government which ruled with an iron fist, for it does not aim to rest for its security on the consent of the governed." Advocating this kind of government was "a vicious doctrine, subversive to our institutions and menacing the orderly rule of law," but it was not anarchism. If Gitlow or others actually attempted to bring about such change, it would inevitably involve a breach of the peace and other violations. Pound and Cardozo agreed with the majority that the New York legislature was the proper authority to determine what an abuse of the right of free speech was. But that fact did not justify winking at a conviction under an inapplicable law. "Although the defendant may be the worst of men, the rights of the best of men are secure only as the rights of the worst and most abhorrent are protected."

The appeals process produced very little that was useful to the ACLU, let alone Gitlow. The court of appeals—dissenters as well as majority—rejected almost without comment the speech-rights argument of the defense. The dissenters simply thought a law against anarchist doctrine should be limited to anarchists. No judge on any level agreed that the New York legislature had stepped outside constitutional bounds in passing the criminal anarchy law. The argument that the due process clause of the Fourteenth Amendment expanded speech protection beyond that provided by the New York Constitution was barely addressed at all. The First Amendment itself got almost no mention. The Winnipeg testimony stood. And although some of the judges seriously considered whether a political tract that did not directly incite or call for illegal acts could be criminal, they all decided that it could. That set the stage for the test of peacetime sedition laws in the Supreme Court that the ACLU was aiming for and to which a somewhat reluctant but game Gitlow had acceded.

The Time to Kill a Snake

The *Gitlow* case reached the Supreme Court in April 1923. The ACLU must have known its chances for a favorable ruling were small by a simple nose count. In all the speech cases that had come before the Court since the beginning of World War I, only one justice other than Oliver Wendell Holmes and Louis Brandeis had ever voted to overturn a conviction, and that was a single time on narrow grounds. Although briefs written by Gitlow's lawyers at each step of the appeals process argued that a peacetime sedition conviction would be a novel and radical departure from established practice, in fact, it would be neither; it was a logical, almost inescapable extension of the bad tendency doctrine.

So why would the ACLU risk an appeal when it knew the Court would likely issue a resounding statement in support of peacetime sedition laws? ACLU publications stressed the need for a definitive verdict, despite having little hope it would go their way. The status quo was not a favorable one; since 1917, more than thirty states had enacted some version of a criminal syndicalist or red flag law, some more sweeping than New York's 1902 law. There were also small indications that a more favorable verdict was conceivable. The Red Scare of 1919 had largely subsided. Al Smith's pardons of the other criminal anarchy defendants had hardly created a murmur. Of the Lusk Committee recommendations the New York legislature had written into law, one had been overturned as unconstitutional by the court of appeals in 1922, and the others were repealed by Smith and the legislature, also with no public fanfare. Nationally, the star of A. Mitchell Palmer, Wilson's attorney general and namesake of the Palmer raids, had fallen so far that he was now considered a political liability for Democrats; in fact, James Cox, the 1920 Democratic presidential nominee, had refused Palmer's offer to campaign for him. Warren

Harding had commuted Eugene Debs's sentence to time served. Although state courts generally upheld sedition laws, there was a glimmer of hope on that front too. In 1920 the Supreme Court of California had overturned the conviction of a woman arrested for displaying a red flag at a meeting, holding that California's ban on symbols suggesting "theories of government antagonistic to the Constitution and laws of the United States" was too broad (*ex parte Hartman*). In 1921 the Supreme Court of New Jersey had overturned the conviction of a Communist Party of America member for advocating the overthrow of the government, on the grounds that the only evidence against him consisted of statements of Marxist principles he had made to the police after his arrest (*State of New Jersey v. Gabriel*). The conviction of Gitlow associate Israel Amter, arrested for carrying a stack of Communist pamphlets, had also been overturned because "possession of an unopened package of Communist Party pamphlets does not constitute a violation of the [criminal anarchy] law." These decisions were only a small judicial countercurrent, but they indicated some limits on sedition prosecutions.

The task for the ACLU lawyers arguing the *Gitlow* case would be to expand on these libertarian slivers and try to package them into a broader doctrine the Court might accept. Their path to doing that was blocked by two enormous obstacles — the bad tendency test, and the fact that Gitlow had been convicted under state, not federal, law. It was also haunted by a third doctrine — the concept of "liberty of contract," which was not an overt part of this case but bedeviled every step leading up to it. These three elements were so intertwined in the Supreme Court's consideration of speech rights that a change in the Court's stance on any one of them would have an impact on the other two.

————

Speech and Harm

David Rabban, the leading historian of pre–World War I speech rights, described the standing of the First Amendment at that point as one of "judicial hostility and neglect." Oliver Wendell Holmes, before his consequential change of heart, talked about freedom of speech as being no different from "freedom from vaccination" — that is, a provisional liberty easily overridden when the broader interests of the community required it. In fact, there was barely a nod toward any particularity of speech that might separate it from any other harm a community might want to prohibit.

The earliest American formulation of the rights of speech and press drew from English legal theorist William Blackstone and was located at the far — most restrictive — corner of the bad tendency grid. To Blackstone, "free" speech meant that it could not be prohibited before being aired. But speakers and writers were answerable for "abuses" of that right after the fact, and an abuse would be defined by popular majorities through legislatures. The clause in the New York Constitution on speech rights was a condensation of the Blackstone principles. The lawyers for the state at every point in the *Gitlow* case cited that clause so often that it led to a frustrated outburst by Nelles: "It does not advance the inquiry to say that a citizen 'may be held responsible for the *abuse* of the right of free speech' or that the freedom of speech 'does not mean unbridled license.'"

Leonard Levy wrote an influential book arguing that passage of the First Amendment was only meant to codify the Blackstone "no prior restraint" doctrine. He later modified that claim and demonstrated that through the debates over the Sedition Act of 1798, a more libertarian strain of thinking emerged. James Madison argued during the Sedition Act conflict that "some abuse is inseparable from the proper use of everything" and that getting the benefit of free discussion required tolerating the inevitable abuses. But it is just as certain that some of the Sedition Act's supporters did subscribe to the narrow understanding of the First Amendment that Levy described. One of those supporters wrote to his constituents, "The words 'freedom of speech' mean, in their true technical import, an exemption from any control previous to its publication," leaving the speaker "answerable for the abuse of that liberty." This "true technical" — that is, Blackstonian — definition left speech as open to regulation by temporary majorities as any other "harmful" activity.

Although the Blackstone and bad tendency doctrines are compatible, they are not identical. The view that government is free to punish the abuse of speech as long as it was not subject to prior restraint leaves open the definition of *abuse*. The bad tendency doctrine fills in that gap. If it can be argued that a speaker's words might plausibly

{ *Chapter 6* }

cause an unspecified listener to commit a criminal act sometime in the future, the speaker has abused the right of speech and can be charged with a crime. The sole difference between harm by words and harm by robbery is that words cannot be penalized until after their appearance. After speech has been committed, any punishment goes. The bad tendency doctrine simply adds a requirement that the prosecution specify the harm that might be caused by the words. That was the point of the Winnipeg testimony in the criminal anarchy trials. The state argued — accurately — that Gitlow hoped readers would try to bring about a Winnipeg-like situation in New York. Gitlow was thus responsible for the crime of urging readers to commit illegal acts of the kind being committed in Winnipeg.

The Supreme Court put its stamp of approval on the bad tendency doctrine in *U.S. ex rel. Turner v. Williams* (1904). The New York criminal anarchy law was one response to the McKinley assassination; the federal government also weighed in by prohibiting "anarchists or persons who believe in or advocate the overthrow by force or violence of the government of the United States" from visiting the country on even a temporary basis. John Turner, a visiting British labor organizer and admitted anarchist, was sentenced to deportation under the law, the main evidence against him being favorable comments he had made on use of the general strike. His lawyers fought against deportation on First Amendment grounds. The Supreme Court ruled against Turner, with its main argument being that noncitizens are not entitled to First Amendment protection. But Chief Justice Melville Fuller wanted it understood that Turner would have lost on First Amendment grounds anyway. "The tendency of the general exploration of such [anarchist] views is so dangerous to the public weal" that it did not matter whether anyone might act on Turner's words or whether he intended that they do so. That line appears to have been a response to the argument by Turner's lawyers — echoed in a separate opinion by David Brewer — that the law was questionable because it did not distinguish between "philosophical anarchists" and advocates of "propaganda of the deed." That did not matter, the Court said: Congress had decided that anarchists were dangerous, and "as long as governments endure, they cannot be denied the right of self-preservation." *Turner* appeared regularly in the arguments of the prosecution and the judges in the *Gitlow* case.

Who Shall Make No Law?

The government's inherent "right of self-preservation" was not the only obstacle Gitlow's lawyers faced, and in the end, it was not the issue for which the case earned its reputation. The other problem was just as formidable: the First Amendment applied only to laws passed by the federal government. The phrasing "Congress shall make no law" was not a slip of the Framers' pen. The nationalists who wrote the Constitution had to sell their ideas in a popular climate where suspicion of a distant centralized government was widespread. James Madison, who shepherded the Bill of Rights through the First Congress, found that the guardians of states' rights were just as opposed to a declaration of uniform national rights as they were to central authority. Based on his experience in Virginia, he thought that rights were most likely to be violated by local majorities and therefore urged that the prohibitions on the national government be extended to the states. To Madison, it was the most important proposal; to the defenders of the states, it was the most intrusive and was defeated in the Senate. The defeat of Madison's proposal makes it clear that the First Amendment was intended to prohibit only the federal government from restricting speech or establishing religion. The Supreme Court reemphasized that point in 1845 in *Permoli v. City of New Orleans.* When a Catholic priest tried to use the First Amendment to challenge a fine imposed on him for holding a funeral in his church, in violation of a city health ordinance, the Court reiterated what history had made clear: "The Constitution makes no provision for protecting the citizens of the respective states in their religious liberties." In *Barron v. Baltimore*, Chief Justice John Marshall extended that principle to the other protections in the Bill of Rights. Why would Marshall, the great nationalist, reject national standards in the sphere of rights? The reason may be simply that the historical record was unambiguous. Madison had proposed "no state shall," and the Senate had rejected it.

Passage of the Fourteenth Amendment created new possibilities that the Bill of Rights might be extended to cover state actions. A quick look at the clause prohibiting states from abridging "the privileges and immunities of citizens of the United States" might leave the impression that the Bill of Rights was now applicable to the states. But the Supreme Court stopped that interpretation at the starting line. In the *Slaughterhouse* cases in 1873, a group of Louisiana butchers claimed that the state had interfered with their right to pursue their occupation by creating a single center for the slaughtering of livestock. The lawyers for the butchers went on a fishing expedition in the post–Civil War amendment pond to support that argument. They claimed that Louisiana had violated the Thirteenth Amendment's prohibition on involuntary servitude, as well as the equal protection and due process clauses of the Fourteenth Amendment. The argument they relied on most heavily was that the privileges and immunities clause of the Fourteenth Amendment extended all the protections in the Constitution to citizens in the states. Samuel Miller, speaking for the Court majority, denied all the claims and focused on the privileges and immunities argument (as opposed to the due process claim, which, he said, "was not much pressed"). If he had simply ruled that it was proper for a state to regulate in the field of health, the case would have had no place in the history of the "incorporation" doctrine. But he argued that the purpose of the privileges and immunities clause was mainly to overturn the *Dred Scott* decision; beyond that, it created a new class of national rights so small that he had to describe it to prove it existed: the right to visit the nation's capital, the right to run for national office, the right to have access to seaports and to ensure federal protection at sea. Clearly, the First Amendment need not apply. The butchers' broader interpretation of the Fourteenth Amendment, he wrote, would "fetter and degrade the state governments." Four justices dissented from the decision, but of those, only Justice Joseph Bradley argued explicitly that the privileges and immunities clause had been meant to apply the first eight amendments in the Bill of Rights to the states.

Another dissent in the *Slaughterhouse* cases foreshadowed a different issue that indirectly caused problems for the civil libertarian interpretation of the First Amendment that Gitlow would need on appeal. Stephen Field disagreed with the majority's ultra-narrow construction of the Fourteenth Amendment. But in a lengthy opinion, he did not include the Bill of Rights among the rights protected against state invasion. Instead, he described the privileges and immunities clause as a prohibition against state interference with "a right to pursue one of the ordinary trades or callings in life." The Louisiana law did not prohibit anyone from becoming a butcher, so he clarified that what had been taken away was the right to pursue a trade "unmolested" — that is, without regulation. Field admitted there was no such right enumerated in the Constitution, but he found it implicit in the Declaration of Independence, English history, and the writing of French historians. In *Allgeyer v. Louisiana* (1897), the Court majority gave a name to Field's right — "liberty of contract."

Thus, the Fourteenth Amendment *did* protect rights from state action, but only those regarding the use of property. The Court would soon begin to find more and more constitutional protections against state interference in the free market. In *Chicago, Burlington and Quincy Railroad v. Chicago* (1897), the Court upheld a railroad owners' argument that they could not be forced to sell any part of their property by the state legislature because that would violate the due process clause of the Fifth Amendment, applied to the states by the Fourteenth. The majority seems to have absentmindedly forgotten the *Slaughterhouse* ruling in upholding the owners' claim — in spite of the fact that Justice Miller was still on the Court and voted with the majority.

But there was no similar expansion to individuals of any of the rights enumerated in the Bill of Rights. Miller's ruling that the privileges and immunities clause did not extend any protection against state restrictions was quickly reaffirmed by subsequent decisions, most brusquely in *Walker v. Sauvinet* (1875). Walker, the owner of a coffee shop, had refused service to Sauvinet because he was "a man of color." The judge ordered a finding against Walker when the jury deadlocked, and Walker appealed on the grounds that the judge had violated his Seventh Amendment right to a jury trial. The Supreme Court ruled that Walker had no such right in a state case and again rejected the argument that the privileges and immunities clause extended the coverage of the Bill of Rights. "The States, so far as this amendment is concerned, are left to regulate trials in their own courts in their own way." Field dissented, probably because the Court's decision permitted restrictions on the way an owner conducted his business.

The Court majority slammed the door on the use of the privileges and immunities clause to incorporate the Bill of Rights with such finality that in a Second Amendment case 130 years later, Antonin Scalia ridiculed a lawyer for reraising it. With that means of expanding the protection of individual rights blocked, lawyers retrenched and began to ask the Court to read substantive rights into the due process clause of the Fourteenth Amendment. That door had been left slightly open; Bradley and Noah Swayne had mentioned the due process argument favorably in their individual *Slaughterhouse* dissents, and the majority opinion spent only two paragraphs refuting it, in contrast to twenty-eight on the privileges and immunities argument. In cases in which the due process claim had to do with economic liberty, it was often successful; when a case concerned a Bill of Rights liberty, it was not. The Court's most definitive statement against an interpretation of the due process clause that would incorporate the Bill of Rights came in *Maxwell v. Dow* (1900). An armed robber in Utah had been convicted by an eight-person jury, rather than the twelve needed for a federal charge. The defense argued that this was a violation of the due process clause; the Court disagreed. "The protection of rights of life and personal liberty within the respective states rests alone with the states." The Court majority made no attempt to reconcile that statement with its vigorous defense of economic liberty against state action. John Marshall Harlan dissented, as he often did in Fourteenth Amendment cases, arguing that the Bill of Rights should be extended to the states. "It would seem that the protection of private property is of more consequence than the protection of the life and liberty of citizens."

Finally the Court budged just a little in its refusal to uphold noneconomic liberties. Albert Twining was tried in 1904 in New Jersey for fraudulently reporting bank stock transfers. He declined to testify, and New Jersey law permitted the prosecution and the judge to point to his failure to testify as evidence of guilt. They both did so, and Twining was convicted. His lawyers argued to the Supreme Court that the right against self-incrimination in federal cases should be made applicable to state prosecutions under the due process clause of the Fourteenth Amendment. The Court majority in *Twining v. New Jersey* (1908) admitted for the first time that "it is possible that some of the personal rights safeguarded by the first eight Amendments against national action may also be safeguarded against state action." The Court made it clear that it was not simply extending the Bill of Rights to the states. The only new rights safeguarded were those that "are of such a nature that they are included in the conception of due process of law." The right against self-incrimination was not "of such a nature" to the Court at the time, and Twining lost. The Court gave no examples of what rights it had in mind, and Justice Harlan again dissented, pointing out how murky the Court's position was and urging his simpler solution of declaring that the Fourteenth Amendment nationalized the first eight. But his position was, and still is, a distinct minority view, and the slight movement in *Twining* produced no immediate extension of rights. That was the situation as Gitlow's case moved toward the Supreme Court. The significance was clear. Ben Gitlow had been charged under a New York law, and his lawyers had to confront the problem of the state being permitted to make its own rules in the area of individual liberties before they could engage in any discussion of the interpretation of the First Amendment.

The contribution of the liberty-of-contract debate to eliminate this jigsaw puzzle was indirect but real. When the Court majority invoked that doctrine, it was striking down the actions of legislative majorities, often at the state level. The opponents of liberty of contract had two different counterarguments available. The first was the argument that it was a made-up doctrine, found nowhere in the Constitution. That is what the Court eventually decided in 1937: "the Constitution does not speak of a freedom of contract." But the second path of opposition was initially more compelling. The liberty-of-contract majority was taking what is now called an "activist" position with regard to economic legislation, awarding itself wide powers to strike down the actions of legislative majorities. Many of the justices looked on legislative interference in the free market as guilty until proved innocent. This meant that the opponents of liberty of contract could call for judicial restraint — that is, a strong presumption of the constitutionality of the actions of majorities through their elected officials. These different paths crossed in the famous case of *Lochner v. New York* (1905), concerning the constitutionality of a New York law limiting the hours bakers could be made to work. It was a state case, and it was argued in front of a Supreme Court in which the majority held that the Bill of Rights did not restrain state action. But this case was about economic regulation, on which the same majority took a skeptical and activist position. The Court invalidated the New York law. Harlan disagreed with the majority and based his dissent on the need to grant a presumption of validity to legislation "unless it be beyond, plainly, palpably, beyond all question in excess of legislative power." He was joined by Holmes, who wrote a virtual paean to judicial restraint. "My agreement or disagreement has nothing to do with the right of a majority to embody their opinions in law. . . . [A] constitution is not intended to embody a particular economic theory. . . . [T]he accident of our finding certain opinions natural and familiar or novel and even shocking ought not to conclude our judgment upon the question of whether statutes embodying them conflict with the Constitution of the United States."

This dissent was part of a thirty-year battle Holmes and later Brandeis fought against the liberty-of-contract justices, rooted in the right of majorities, as expressed through their representatives, to be given a wide benefit of the doubt. Holmes once wrote, "I hate a man who knows that he knows," and he translated that into a distrust of justices enacting what they thought they knew through the vehicle of the Fourteenth Amendment. This, not speech rights, was Holmes's great battle during his time on the Court, and some of his First Amendment views cannot be understood outside that context.

The first prominent case in which a state prosecution was contested as a violation of speech rights was *Patterson v. Colorado* (1907), and Holmes wrote the Court's opinion. Patterson was a former senator from Colorado who owned a crusading Populist newspaper. When the Colorado Supreme Court issued a ruling favorable to a state utility company, the newspaper ridiculed the decision. Patterson was convicted of contempt of court for interfering with an ongoing case (ongoing only in the sense that the decision might be appealed). Patterson's appeal of his contempt conviction to the U.S. Supreme Court was based not on the First or Fourteenth Amendment but on the kind of natural rights extrapolation that had often carried the Court in economic liberty cases. The nature of the case forced Holmes to try to assemble the pieces of the ill-fitting jigsaw puzzle of Court doctrine on state speech laws. The Court majority was comfortable with the use of the Fourteenth Amendment to judge state economic laws, but it was unsympathetic to Patterson's claims because they involved speech. Harlan, who dissented in the case, had consistently argued that the privileges and immunities clause was intended to extend the Bill of Rights to the states, but he added that the due process clause could also serve as a basis for overturning Patterson's conviction. Holmes had a difficult choice to make. He might have ruled that the Four-teenth Amendment placed no substantive restrictions on states, but the majority would not have accepted that. He could have joined Har-lan in dissent, but that would have meant accepting a view of the due process clause that he opposed. And there was no reason to believe that in 1908 Holmes agreed with Harlan that the First Amendment protected Patterson's newspaper columns. So he punted. Before there was any substantive discussion of the issues of the case, he noted, "we leave undecided" any applicability of the First Amendment. There was no need to decide this issue, Holmes wrote; even if the First Amend-ment did apply to the states, Patterson had no case. The main purpose of the First Amendment, Holmes wrote, was to prohibit prior restraint, not to "prevent the subsequent punishment of such as may be deemed contrary to the public welfare." Patterson had suffered no prior restraint, since he had obviously published his columns. So the first major speech-rights decision of the century affirmed the Black-stone doctrine and left it to the legislature and the local courts to decide what speech was "contrary to the public welfare."

Holmes and the Court confronted roughly the same set of ques-tions and came to roughly the same conclusions in 1915 in *Fox v. Wash-ington*. Jay Fox's magazine ran an article calling for a boycott of some local businesses whose owners had reported nude bathers to the police. He was convicted under a state law forbidding publications that might "encourage or advocate disrespect for the law [against nudity]." The Washington Supreme Court, in affirming the conviction, discussed the boundaries of the First Amendment. That allowed the U.S. Supreme Court to review the case without making any further com-ment on incorporation. Holmes again wrote the opinion affirming the conviction, arguing that Fox's article "by indirection but unmistak-ably" encouraged people to violate the decency law. The lower courts, he said, had construed the law so that it did not punish mere opposi-tion to the law but only the advocacy of illegal acts, which presumably meant more naked bathing. The smallness of the underlying issue and the improbability that the magazine article could cause an outbreak of nudity demonstrate Holmes's low regard for the First Amendment at that point and make his later rulings more noteworthy.

This was how speech rights stood before the World War I cases began to transform them: no prohibition of state interference (as there was in the area of property rights); no prohibition on penalties for speech that was "contrary to the public welfare," as long as there was no prior restraint; and a bad tendency test in which *bad* was defined by legislative majorities and *tendency* covered as much time as judges and juries could imagine. Over the next several years, the Court would be forced to take stock of those assumptions in a series of prosecutions stemming from the 1917 Espionage Act. Since the vast majority of these cases involved federal charges, the sole question would be the Court's interpretation of the First Amendment itself. The Court entered this period reliant on the mixture of Blackstone and the bad tendency doctrine that had guided previous cases, but there was little in its past that prepared it to deal with the issues emerging from dissent in wartime.

Holmes and Brandeis without Restraint

Charles Schenck and Eugene Debs, leading figures in the Socialist Party (the party Gitlow had left in 1919), were convicted for statements opposing World War I and the draft. Schenck was held responsible for a Socialist leaflet criticizing the war and comparing the draft to involuntary servitude. The leaflet had been mailed to, among others, draft-eligible men. Debs's conviction was based on a speech he gave in Canton, Ohio, in which he condemned the war and capitalism and praised draft evaders he had visited in jail. Both were charged with attempting to obstruct military recruiting, in violation of the Espionage Act. Holmes wrote opinions for a unanimous Court in both cases, upholding the convictions on the grounds that Schenck and Debs had engaged in veiled attempts to encourage draft evasion. He admitted that in Debs's case the "criminal" advocacy was a small part of the whole, but concluded that it was sufficient in wartime for the Court to uphold the conviction. In a letter to Harold Laski, Holmes wrote that he "regretted having to write [these opinions] – and (between ourselves) that the Government had pressed them to a hearing. . . . But on the only question before us, I could not doubt about the law." His North Star was still judicial restraint.

It was in his *Schenck* opinion that Holmes employed the famous phrase "clear and present danger." For all the furor that followed and continues to this day, it is not clear that Holmes meant very much by it. He did not repeat the phrase in the *Debs* opinion that came a week later. Nor did he repeat it in his opinion in *Frohwerk v. United States*, another Espionage Act case released the same day as the *Debs* decision. Jacob Frohwerk edited a small German-language newspaper with a pro-German viewpoint on the war. Holmes noted a "sneering contrast" between English and German leaders and quoted a line from the paper that called it "a monumental and inexcusable mistake to send our soldiers to Germany." He acknowledged that, unlike Schenck, Frohwerk made no effort to send his paper to draft-age men. But he found that its antiwar message might encourage some violation of the Espionage Act. "It is impossible to say that it might not have been found that the circulation of the paper was in quarters where a little breath would be enough to kindle a flame." Could there be a more remote relationship between words and conduct, especially one leading to a ten-year prison sentence?

Holmes's opinions in these cases put him at odds — to his surprise — with some legal progressives, including his British pen pal Harold Laski and future Supreme Court justice Felix Frankfurter. The most important of his critics may have been New York judge Learned Hand, whose opinion in an earlier case pointed in a different direction. In July 1917 Postmaster General Albert Burleson invoked the Espionage Act to prevent the *Masses*, a leftist antiwar magazine, from being distributed through the mail. Though strongly hostile to the war, the magazine did not call for any illegal means of opposition. Hand overturned Burleson's order and temporarily restored the *Masses*' right to use the mail. In doing so, he proposed a standard for speech rights that was significantly wider than the one Holmes would suggest two years later. Hand distinguished between "political agitation" and "direct incitement to violent resistance." While admitting that antiwar "agitation" could, under some circumstances, contribute to lawlessness, it also played a necessary role as "a safeguard of free governments." The test was not whether opposition to the war might lead to criminal acts but whether it directly incited those acts. "The literal meaning is the starting point for interpretation."

Hand's ruling was quickly set aside by the Second Circuit Court, which preferred to look at the "natural and reasonable effect of what is said" rather than the literal meaning. Hand's *Masses* opinion was not cited by anyone in the *Gitlow* appeals, but it gained importance in an indirect way. Hand and Holmes met by accident on a train in June 1918, and from the letters they exchanged afterward, it appears that free speech was the main topic of conversation. Following the *Schenck*, *Debs*, and *Frohwerk* decisions, Hand wrote to Holmes and suggested that his own "direct incitement" test would have led to different, and better, decisions. Holmes responded that he did not see any difference between Hand's test and his own in *Schenck*, and he added that he would have reached a different conclusion from Hand's in the *Masses* case. Holmes was intrigued, but initially unmoved, by the critique of his Espionage Act opinions from former allies.

Then he changed course. He denied it was a change, but it was. The next significant speech-rights case was *Abrams v. New York*, involving three anarchists and a Socialist convicted for distributing a leaflet opposing American intervention in Russia following the revolution. The Court majority upheld the conviction based on reasoning that was similar to Holmes's opinions in previous cases: the leafletters called for a strike in munitions plants that, though wildly improbable, would have had the indirect effect of limiting production for the broader war. Thus, the majority reasoned, the defendants' "intent" was to impede the war effort. But this time, Holmes wrote a landmark dissent. He began by repeating his belief that *Schenck* and *Debs* had been decided correctly, and it is true that some of the facts in *Abrams* were different. First, the leafletters had much less public visibility than Debs and Schenck. Second, they were protesting not World War I but the occupation of Russia, with which the United States was not at war. And finally, they had been convicted under the more constitutionally questionable Sedition Act amendments of 1918, not the original Espionage Act. But if the tone and emotive force of words mean anything, the Holmes dissent in *Abrams* was an enormous departure from his previous opinions.

He provided a new and less malleable meaning for the nebulous "clear and present danger" standard: to be punishable, speech must so "imminently threaten immediate interference" with lawful activities that an "immediate check" was required. Six months of reflection and interaction with critics of his prior decisions had turned conjecture about what Frohwerk's newspaper might have done at some future point into a requirement that the threat be imminent. The demand for a much closer relation in time and place between speech and criminal activity was Holmes's practical challenge to the prevailing bad tendency doctrine. But his dissent's greater long-term influence lay in his evoking the language of John Stuart Mill, whom Holmes had heard lecture in England as a young man. The most famous lines in the *Abrams* dissent were clearly derived from Mill and rooted in the concept of human fallibility. "When men have realized that time has upset many fighting faiths, they may come to believe even more than they believe the very foundations of their own conduct that the ultimate good desired is better reached by free trade in ideas." Holmes has been criticized in recent years for proposing the protection of only ineffectual speech, and in another part of his dissent, he did call the anarchists "puny anonymities." But the Mill-influenced backdrop of this dissent set the tone for the expansion of the First Amendment over the next eighty years.

Brandeis had previously been even more dismissive of speech rights than Holmes, later admitting, "I thought at the subject, not through it." This time, he joined the dissent. From that point on, he and Holmes voted together to uphold First Amendment claims fourteen times, including twelve dissents. They voted on opposite sides only once. Unfortunately for Gitlow's lawyers, that was in a case with some similar features: *Gilbert v. Minnesota* (1920).

Joseph Gilbert was a Socialist leader of the Non-Partisan League in Minnesota, which blended populist rhetoric with criticism of the war. The state had a large German population, ensuring a sympathetic audience for the League's antiwar message. The state legislature passed its own version of the Espionage Act, making it a crime to write or print "that the citizens of this state should not aid or assist the United States in prosecuting or carrying on war with the public enemies of the United States." Gilbert was charged with violating the state law after giving an antiwar speech at a public meeting. The closest he came to advocating draft resistance were these words: "If this is a good democracy, for Heaven sake why should we not vote on conscription? . . . [I]f they conscripted wealth like they conscripted men, this war would not last twenty four hours." This was enough to ensure conviction under the vague Minnesota law.

The Supreme Court upheld the conviction over dissents by Brandeis and Chief Justice Edward Douglass White. White's objection was brief and limited to his concern that Congress had preempted the field of laws dealing with wartime dissent. Joseph McKenna's majority opinion read more like a rant than a judicial statement. He warmed up with a response to White on preemption: Minnesota had a right to pass its own law because the success of the war depended on "the morale, the spirit and determination that animates" the citizenry. The government had a right to public opinion that was "eager and militant" rather than "repellent and adverse." Minnesota's law was a useful addition to the cheerleading. Then, on the issue of speech rights itself, he said it was a "strange perversion" that the Constitution was being used to "justify the activities of anarchy or the enemies of the United States." This insistence on rights for war protesters had come up before, he wrote, and the Court had not only rejected that argument but also warned everyone not to raise it again: "We forestalled all repetitions of it and the case at bar is a repetition of it." Gilbert had criticized a war that was "in defense of our national honor," and "every word that Gilbert uttered in denunciation of the war was false." Finding in favor of Gilbert would be "a travesty on the constitutional privilege he invokes." McKenna's opinion was deservedly characterized in an ACLU memo as "an assertion of naked power, avowedly guided by emotion."

Brandeis wrote in complete and vigorous opposition to the majority decision, but he had to walk a fine line. On the one hand, he disagreed wholeheartedly with McKenna's interpretation of speech rights and the duties and obligations of citizens in wartime, stating, "in frank expression of opinion lies the greatest promise of wisdom." On the other hand, this was a state case, and he would have to explain why the Supreme Court should rule on it without conceding wide-ranging powers to a Court whose majority was still committed to Fourteenth Amendment activism in the economic realm, which he opposed. McKenna declined to address whether the claimed Fourteenth Amendment protection for speech actually existed, modeled on the way Holmes had finessed *Patterson* and *Fox*. In McKenna's view, Gilbert had no claim under any interpretation of speech rights, making it unnecessary to say whether the due process clause offered protection for speech. Brandeis tried to tap-dance around the problem. First, he agreed with White that the national Espionage Act preempted state action; in fact, he gave a passing salute to the Espionage

Act as more protective of speech than the Minnesota law ("The federal act did not prohibit the teaching of any doctrine; it prohibited only certain tangible obstructions"). Then he pointed out that although this was a state law, the war was a national issue. "The right to speak freely concerning functions of the federal government is a privilege or immunity of every citizen of the United States." But knowing that his dissent would have limited value if it applied only to national issues, and knowing that the "privileges and immunities" route to extend rights to states was blocked, he had to bite the bullet and invoke the due process clause. Near the end of successive drafts of his dissent, he wrote a one-sentence note to himself: "I cannot believe that the liberty guaranteed by the Fourteenth Amendment included only liberty to acquire and to enjoy property." That sentence, which seemed to be a backhanded concession to the liberty-of-contract majority, must have been difficult for Brandeis to write. It did not appear in the next draft, but he did insert it in the second to last draft, in a different typeface, making it clear that adding it had been a last-minute decision. It became the final line of his dissent.

If it was difficult for Brandeis, it must have been impossible for Holmes, who had been battling the Fourteenth Amendment activists since he joined the Court. His comments on the case are cryptic. He wrote a note to Brandeis saying, "You go too far," without specifying how. In a letter to Frederick Pollock, he wrote that Brandeis "had one ground worthy of serious consideration and others that I thought were wrong — while I heartily disagreed with the majority." He did not specify which was which. But in a letter to Felix Frankfurter, he mentioned a previous liberty-of-contract case in the context of a discussion of *Gilbert* and pointed to his opinion advocating judicial restraint. In a record of a conversation with Frankfurter about the *Gilbert* decision, Brandeis noted, "Holmes says doesn't want to extend XIV." In other words, Holmes was too committed to his long battle for a narrower interpretation of the Fourteenth Amendment to join Brandeis's dissent in *Gilbert*.

Their difference on *Gilbert* is sometimes used to argue that Brandeis had a more expansive and democratic view of speech rights than Holmes did. It is true that Holmes later adopted Brandeis's thinking on state cases and that Brandeis's *Gilbert* dissent eventually became accepted Court doctrine. But if there had been any substantial disagreement between them, they would not have signed each other's dissents so often. *Gilbert* demonstrated that they were fully capable of taking different sides if their conclusions were different. Holmes later wrote that he was glad there was disagreement on *Gilbert* because "it shows them there is no pre-established harmony." The extent of their agreement was impressive; they ruled on the same side of every speech-rights case during their time on the Court, with this one exception. But in this case, Holmes was looking backward to an old (though not nearly dead) debate about economic regulation, while Brandeis was looking ahead to the nationalization of the Bill of Rights.

The Role of Circumstances

Walter Nelles and Walter Pollak, who drafted Gitlow's application for a writ of error to the Supreme Court, must have known that Brandeis and especially Holmes were reluctant to endorse wide powers for the Court through the use of the Fourteenth Amendment. But they were also the only two justices whose sympathy for the lawyers' position on speech rights seemed likely. In the original submission for a writ, Nelles left blank the line indicating which clause of the Constitution was at issue. Brandeis reviewed the writ and "expressed doubt whether on this state of the record the constitutional question was properly raised." He referred the application to the full Court. Faced with hesitation by the one judge who was almost certain to be on his side, Nelles amended the petition to specify that the constitutional issue was the due process clause of the Fourteenth Amendment. The New York Court of Appeals amended its own decision, inserting a statement that the Fourteenth Amendment had been "considered and passed on by this Court." Both the defense and the appeals court itself wanted a higher court ruling.

The state of New York predictably did not. In a memorandum opposing a writ of error, New York attorney general Charles Newton wrote that neither the First nor the Fourteenth Amendment "ever contemplated the authorization to publish, either by word of mouth or in writing, anything which would advocate the assassination of public officials or the destruction of the government, state or national. . . . The petitioner-in-error sought to destroy the very constitution under whose protective wing he now seeks shelter. He ought not to be heard to complain." But this was inherently an argument that should be heard by the Court. There was one issue that might have kept the case out of the Court's reach altogether. In *Prudential Insurance Co. v. Cheek*, decided shortly before the Court weighed whether to take *Gitlow*, the majority opinion included this comment. "The Constitution of the United States imposes upon the states no obligation to confer upon those within their jurisdiction either the right of free speech or the right of silence." Newton could have argued that with this statement the Court had ruled against the incorporation doctrine unambiguously. Nelles knew the ruling was a problem and filed a three-page addendum to his brief, trying to differentiate that case from Gitlow's. But Newton did not mention *Prudential*, and the Court agreed to hear the case.

Stewardship of the *Gitlow* case had shifted from the leftist lawyers Hale and Recht to the ACLU lawyers Nelles and Pollak. The background music for the free-speech arguments raised by the leftists had been of the "prophet dishonored in his own time" type. That had been the theme of Darrow's defense, and it was present in more muted form in the appeals briefs written by Recht and Hale. Pollak's brief made it clear that the substance of the "Left Wing Manifesto" would play no role in his argument. "Our contention is that the statute, prohibiting advocacy as such, without a showing of circumstances in which it is properly punishable, is unconstitutional. We do not, therefore, discuss the construction of the Manifesto." His only reference to the language of the manifesto was to point to the appeals court's stipulation that it contained no advocacy of illegal acts. Other than that, Pollak put aside any discussion of what ideas or acts the manifesto was advocating.

His case would be tightly wrapped around one point: "the statute penalizes doctrine as doctrine, without regard to consequences or to the proximate likelihood of consequences." He began with an extended exploration of English and early American concepts of seditious libel—the crime of attacking the government with words. His thesis was that the original American understanding of civil liberties had been created in direct opposition to the prevailing legal culture in England, which accepted the validity of the doctrine of seditious libel. The moral of this historical story was that a revolution rooted in opposition to British practices and that gave rise to the natural rights language of the Declaration of Independence must have been motivated by great sympathy for the freedom to express doctrines of political disaffection. "It was not only natural, but perhaps inevitable that American independence should establish a broad liberty of political doctrine."

Pollak understood, of course, that the most he could get out of this history was the suggestion that Americans valued liberty and sometimes protected it. Then why devote so much of the brief to it? There were two possible motives. There was an outside chance he could reach some of the liberty-of-contract justices, who sometimes invoked the Declaration of Independence in interpreting the Fourteenth Amendment. To that end, he even made a favorable reference to *Allgeyer* — the quintessential liberty-of-contract case — as the kind of decision that could be deduced from the general concept of liberty contained in the Declaration. His other motive was more realistic: to equip those who were inclined to be supportive of speech rights — Holmes and Brandeis on this Court, and others in the future — with a useful package of history. Pollak drew this conclusion: "It is unthinkable that men who not only asserted but acted upon such principles could carry over into a government based upon them a principle of English law under which mere advocacy was a crime." There would be echoes of Pollak's words in Brandeis's famous *Whitney* opinion two years later.

Pollak certainly could not have imagined that such broad generalizations from history would give the Court sufficient reason to overturn the verdict. So he also created a favorable narrative from the Court's own recent speech-rights decisions. He wove an argument — a fairy tale, really — that in each of these cases the circumstances determined the outcome. Pollak's reason for reinventing the cases this way was straightforward: the *Gitlow* prosecutors had never alleged that the message of the "Left Wing Manifesto" was likely to cause anything to happen. The *way* he did it involved sleight of hand. His takeoff point was Holmes's declaration in *Schenck* that "every case must be decided by the nature of the circumstances." He emphasized that Holmes had said "every case" and argued that the Court had done exactly that in its decisions from *Fox* through *Gilbert*. The nature of all these cases, he wrote, "involved primarily an analysis of the circumstances of publication." The Holmes-Brandeis dissents that began with *Abrams* were simply disagreements about the nature of the circumstances. What bound together all the post-*Schenck* decisions, he argued, "was the emergency of war." The centerpiece of Court reasoning, in Pollak's reconstruction of it, was that "guilt may not rest upon the fact of publication alone — [but] upon the danger inherent in the quality of the words used. It is in the light of surrounding circumstances that the danger of publication is to be tested." Pollak knew this was a reach. *Fox* had nothing to do with circumstances. The Court had ruled that Jay Fox's article might lead to disrespect for a law, not that it was likely to incite mass public nudity. Some of the World War I cases involved tepid antiwar speech — *Gilbert*, for example — and the only emergency the war posed was that the United States was involved in one. In *Frohwerk*, the Court had found that although no special circumstances had been mentioned, the possibility of their existence sometime, somewhere could not be ruled out — hardly a decision that leaned on circumstances.

Holmes's pre-*Abrams* opinions have been criticized for applying the law of criminal attempts to speech cases, thus denying any unique role for the First Amendment. Speech was to criminal acts what the planning of a burglary was to carrying one out — "a question of proximity and degree." But here, Pollak actually encouraged the Court to apply the law of attempts. The prosecution and the majority ruling at each lower level had rejected the requirement of demonstrating proximity and degree. Most important, the criminal anarchy law itself had no such requirement — the advocacy of anarchy was always a crime.

Pollak understood that he was not proposing a doctrine that was highly protective of speech. He left open the possibility that prosecutors or judges could supply the missing circumstances. He also made it clear that he was not asking the Court to go as far in protecting political speech as it had in *Reynolds* in protecting religious speech. In his summary he called explicitly for a "balancing test," a term now anathema to civil libertarians. He even accepted a basic premise of the bad tendency doctrine — that speech causes acts: "When they occasion a substantial evil that the legislature has a right to prevent, the speaker of the language which causes it may be punished."

Pollak's reason for making these concessions was the obvious one: it was the best chance to win the case for his client. There was a much greater likelihood of convincing the Court majority that its prior standards would not sustain the *Gitlow* conviction than of converting three more justices to the position advocated by Holmes and Brandeis. If Pollak succeeded in convincing the majority to apply a balancing test, it would be hard to uphold the conviction because there was nothing to put on the "likely to cause an illegal act" side of the scale. A *New Republic* essay on the case noted that if some agitator read the "Left Wing Manifesto" to a street crowd, it would "disperse them faster than the riot act."

There were two defense briefs — one by John Caldwell Myers and the other by Carl Sherman, the state attorney general. Sherman made the first explicit claim that there was no federal issue because states could make their own rules on speech. "The first amendment was purely a limitation on the power of Congress and that limitation has not been extended to the States by the fourteenth amendment." Myers confronted the "circumstances" argument in his brief. He differentiated between expression that is punishable only when it is "made under such circumstances as to incite the hearers to do that which the law forbids" and "per se abuses of the right of free speech," which are judged inherently harmful. The *Gitlow* case was in the second category. Criminal anarchy, Myers wrote, "is a dangerous doctrine at *any* time." Any government has a fundamental right to self-preservation (one of many references to *Turner*), and the New York legislature had designated the advocacy of criminal anarchy as a threat to public order. His response to Pollak's speech-rights argument was curt: "The brief for the plaintiff-in-error contains a very interesting discussion — much of it historical, much of it philosophical — of the right of free speech. We shall not discuss that question at all."

Sherman went even further. He pointed out that the criminal anarchy law had been passed in the aftermath of the McKinley assassination and that no unusual circumstances surrounded that event: "there was no public unrest; there was no state of war; there were no great strikes or riots in progress." But someone influenced by anarchist ideas had assassinated McKinley "because he represented government." Emma Goldman had placed dangerous ideas in the head of Leon Czolgosz, and the state legislature had responded by making the views of Goldman — and now Gitlow — criminal. "It is the height of folly to punish only the unthinking perpetrator of the crime after it has been committed and let the real criminal, the instigator of the crime who has brought about such a state of mind in some of his less well balanced hearers or readers as to make such a crime possible."

Myers added one final argument if the others failed: "'Imminent' does not necessarily mean the next moment." Gitlow and his associates were "taking definite steps" to bring about these illegal ends, even if they involved no current overt illegal action. These steps included winning converts to the view that the government had to be overthrown. If they convinced enough people, the plan would be unstoppable. Gitlow's teachings were part and parcel of the overthrowing of democratic institutions. Myers summarized the argument in a sentence that could be bad tendency scripture: "The time to kill a snake is when it is young."

A Single Revolutionary Spark

Gitlow was argued on April 12, 1923, and reargued at the Court's request on November 23 of the same year. The decision was not handed down until June 8, 1925. There is no record explaining why it took so long or why it was reargued. The final vote—seven to two in favor of upholding the conviction—was exactly what could have been predicted. The reason for the delay may have been practical. There was a change of Court personnel before the verdict was delivered— Harlan Stone replaced McKenna, although it was McKenna who voted in *Gitlow*. Also, the Court was considering another case at the same time that it might have regarded as more important in redefining federal-state relations (*Meyer v. Nebraska*). Nonetheless, it appears that the justices were debating *Gitlow* until less than a month before the decision was rendered, and the majority opinion and Holmes's dissent were not finalized until the last moment.

The majority opinion was written by Edward Sanford, who had joined the Court just prior to the case. Unlike the justice he replaced, Mahlon Pitney, he was not committed to the liberty-of-contract doctrine and joined Holmes's dissent in one of the important cases in that vein, *Adkins v. Children's Hospital*. Sanford had not been involved in the World War I cases, and his opinion in *Gitlow* seems to have been an effort to find a new basis for resolving speech-rights controversies, although he wound up in the same general place as the previous majorities.

There were two separate and important verdicts in the majority opinion, one consisting of 344 lines and the other consisting of 6. The 344 lines were an interesting addition to the development of judicial reasoning on the First Amendment. The 6 lines are the reason *Gitlow* is still widely cited and discussed: "For present purposes, we may and do assume that freedom of speech and of the press — which are protected by the First Amendment from abridgement by Congress — are among the fundamental personal rights and 'liberties' protected by the due process clause of the Fourteenth Amendment from impairment by the states."

Sanford added that the "incidental" statement to the contrary in the *Prudential* case a year earlier (written by Pitney, whom he replaced) was not "determinative of this question." His somewhat casual declaration, made with little fanfare, is generally regarded as the beginning of the incorporation of the Bill of Rights. Some general statement to that effect had to be included to permit the Court to rule on this case, but it did not have to be as dramatic as the one Sanford made. *Twining* had suggested that some fundamental rights might be contained in the notion of due process that applied to the states. But that ruling had made it clear that these rights would be "of such a nature" that they were included in the concept of due process; they would not be taken from the Bill of Rights. Here, Sanford named the First Amendment as the source of the rights protected from state action, rather than relying on vaguer phraseology about the fundamental nature of speech and press rights.

Because Sanford prefaced his declaration with "For present purposes," some have maintained that *Gitlow* has no special place in the evolution of incorporation. The Court had, of course, ruled on other state speech-rights cases, most notably *Patterson* and *Fox*. Holmes's position in those cases (for the Court) was superficially similar to the stance Sanford adopted here: since the First Amendment would not help the defendant anyway, the Court should explain why and hold the question of the First and Fourteenth Amendments in abeyance. But there is a difference between saying (paraphrasing), "Suppose for a minute that the First Amendment applies to state action. It wouldn't help you anyway," and saying that, at least for this case, the Court assumes that it does apply. The first does not imply that the incorporation doctrine is legitimate; it simply tells the defendant that he cannot expect any help from it. The second is an announcement that the First Amendment does apply, with the recognition that there may be argument on the issue in future cases. The latter is much more likely to be regarded as a precedent, and within five years, it was.

Why did the majority so casually commit itself to such a path-breaking course? There is little to go by. Sanford never commented on it. It may be that the majority was so eager to demonstrate its support of Gitlow's conviction that the justices were willing to go along with any excuse to rule on the case. But that does not explain why the opinion did not rely on the thinner "so what if it did?" language of *Patterson* and *Fox*. Holmes may have provided a clue when he wrote to his British friend Harold Laski two days after the case was first argued: "I am curious to see what the enthusiasts for liberty of contract will say with regard to liberty of speech under a state law punishing advocating the overthrow of government by violence." The liberty-of-contract enthusiasts had a problem that was the mirror opposite of the one Holmes and, to a lesser extent, Brandeis had with *Gilbert*. Their highest goal was not to stop leftists from speaking but to stop the government from regulating. If that meant a passing concession on the meaning of the Fourteenth Amendment in a speech case — one in which the conviction would be upheld anyway — it would be worth it.

The better question is why Holmes accepted this course. Brandeis had already (in his final sentence in *Gilbert*) made his reluctant peace with the tactical need to meet the liberty-of-contract justices halfway on the scope of the Fourteenth Amendment. Holmes had not, and he did not here. One of the ironies of this case is that if Holmes's dissent had been the majority opinion, it would have left a more restrictive view of the First and Fourteenth Amendments in place, and *Gitlow* would not have become a precedent for incorporation. Whereas Sanford stated that, at least for this case, he would assume that the First Amendment's protection of speech applied equally to the states, Holmes proposed a more ambiguous version. He agreed that the "general principle of free speech" should be included in the Fourteenth Amendment, but then qualified it: states should have a "somewhat larger latitude of interpretation than is allowed to Congress." The "larger latitude" was not a concession to the majority; it was a concession to his own reservations about judicial activism through the vehicle of the due process clause. This was a last stand on that issue (as it applied to speech rights) for Holmes; after *Gitlow*, he overcame his qualms about applying the same standards to state and federal cases and never again argued for larger latitude for the states. But if *Gitlow* was a milestone for applying the Bill of Rights to the states, it was done with some trepidation on the part of Holmes.

Although the declaration of incorporation provided civil libertarians with one victory in this case, the substance of the majority opinion provided none at all. It gave no ground on Pollak's free-speech claims, and in one respect, it made matters worse. It began with a summary of facts about Gitlow and the manifesto. Then Sanford added: "There was no evidence of any effect resulting from the publication and circulation of the Manifesto." This was not just an admission of fact; it was crucial to Sanford's opinion. From the beginning of the criminal anarchy cases, the defense had argued that the "Left Wing Manifesto" was not directly counseling anything illegal. Conversely, the prosecution's argument had been that the central purpose of the manifesto was to gain enough adherents to do something massively illegal as soon as possible – to overthrow the government by political strikes. Both portrayals were accurate. Sanford's goal was to find a constitutional formula that admitted the truth of both and sustained the conviction.

He began by merging present and future. The manifesto's plan was to bring about mass strikes like those in Winnipeg. Mass strikes "necessarily imply the use of force and violence; and in their essential nature are inherently unlawful." Therefore, to advocate such a plan, even though the manifesto did not encourage anyone to start striking, was "action to that end." So the "fervent language" with which the manifesto urged people to join in preparing for this future action was criminal. "It is the language of incitement," Sanford stated. The word *incitement* had been part of the World War I speech-rights debates, but with a different meaning than implied here. Learned Hand in the *Masses* case had argued that the government could prohibit only "direct incitement" to illegal action. Hand's incitement standard was much more protective of speech than the Supreme Court was in those years, and Sanford likely knew that. So he appropriated the term and spun it in the opposite direction — *incitement* in his terms meant advocacy that might bring about illegal acts at some point in the future.

That was a long way from "clear and present danger," regardless of the ambiguity of Holmes's famous phrase. Sanford felt that he had to engage that phrase and, in doing so, respond to Pollak's argument about "circumstances." His explanation was clear enough. The war cases had involved violations of the Espionage Act, in which Congress had designated certain acts, such as supplying sensitive information to the enemy or obstructing recruiting, as crimes. The judgments of the courts involved how directly the defendants had counseled the commission of any of those acts — that was what the phrase "clear and present danger" referred to. Both the lower courts and the Supreme Court granted wide latitude for prosecutions, but the basis of all these cases was an allegation that a defendant had urged people to commit the crimes described in the Espionage Act. This case was different. The New York legislature had made a doctrine, not an act, illegal. Sanford wrote that a legislative judgment in the interest of public safety carried a strong presumption of validity. So if a charge involved publication of the banned doctrine, the courts had no role in applying a clear and present danger test or, in fact, any test at all. The legislature had already determined that the doctrine was a crime. "The question whether any specific utterance coming within the prohibited class is likely, in and of itself, to bring about the substantive evil, is not open to consideration." Sanford did not disagree with Pollak that this case was a departure from the prior speech-rights cases, but he drew the opposite conclusion: in this case, the legislature had taken the issue of circumstances off the table.

Sanford's reliance on legislative determination has been described as a creative effort toward a more sensible speech-rights doctrine. But it can just as easily be seen as the basis for permitting wider censorship, as long as it was done by legislatures. The "incorporation" part of the ruling put the same restraints on state action as on congressional action, so in essence, "Congress shall make no law" became "state legislatures shall make no law." The idea that the legislature should be allowed to choose which doctrines are inherently criminal seems directly at odds with that. One way of looking at the Court's expansion of speech protection over the next fifty years is that it gradually reduced the distance between words and the illegal acts needed to make the words criminal. In the World War I cases, the distance (as in the *Frohwerk* case) could be as long as the imagination. Sanford was offering a different approach. A legislature could determine in advance which words "by their very nature involve danger to the public peace." The distance between the appearance of those words and any consequences was immaterial.

Sanford also adopted the essence of Myers's "kill the snake when it is young" theory, although he changed pestilences. "And the immediate danger is none the less real and substantial, because the effect of a given utterance cannot be accurately foreseen. The State cannot reasonably be required to measure the danger of every such utterance in the nice balance of a jeweler's scale. A single, revolutionary spark may kindle a fire that, smoldering for a time, may burst into a sweeping and destructive conflagration." Fire is the perfect metaphor for the bad tendency doctrine, and it was part of the language in the *Gitlow* case from the Magistrate's Court on up. Once started, fire spreads quickly, threatens everything, and does not respond to argument. The civil libertarians involved in Gitlow's defense argued at every turn that if speech is not likely to lead to immediate illegal acts, there is time for other thoughts and counsel to prevent the acts from occurring. Speech, even when expressed in "fervent language," translates into behavior only with additional time. But the Court's majority saw speech through the lens of fire, which consumes immediately. They concluded that it was proper — obligatory — for the state to "extinguish the spark without waiting until it has enkindled the flame or blazed into the conflagration."

Ten Words from Holmes

Shortly after Holmes wrote his dissent, he explained how he felt about the case in a letter to Frederick Pollock: "The theme is one on which I have written majority and minority opinions heretofore and to which I thought I could add about ten words to what I have said before." His dissent in *Gitlow* was a quick restatement of the differences he and Brandeis had had with the majority since the *Abrams* case, with only a nod at some of the particulars. Shortly after the decision was released, he sent Pollock a synopsis, saying he had dissented "in favor of the rights of an anarchist (so-called) to talk drool in favor of the proletarian dictatorship."

The fact that Holmes saw this opinion largely as a reprise helps explain some of the generalizations in it. He reiterated that he and Brandeis had been at odds with the majority since *Abrams*, but "the convictions I expressed in that case are too deep for it to be possible for me to as yet believe that it . . . [has] settled the law." The proper test, Holmes said, was whether the "Left Wing Manifesto" counseled an immediate revolutionary uprising, and no one arguing the state's case had ever claimed that it did. "It is manifest that there was no present danger of an attempt to overthrow the Government by force on the part of the admittedly small minority who shared the defendant's views." He described the conditions under which he might have considered upholding the conviction, emphasizing the time frame:

> If the publication of this document had been laid as an attempt to induce an uprising against government at once and not at some indefinite time in the future it would have presented a different question. The object would have been one with which the law might deal, subject to the doubt whether there was any danger that the publication could produce any result, or in other words, whether it was not futile and too remote from possible consequences. But the indictment alleges the publication and nothing more.

The most impassioned part of Holmes's dissent was his disagreement with Sanford's characterization of the "Left Wing Manifesto" as "incitement." "Every idea is an incitement. It offers itself for belief and if believed it is acted on unless some other belief outweighs it or some failure of energy stifles the movement at its birth. The only difference between an expression of opinion and an incitement in the narrower sense is the speaker's enthusiasm for the result. Eloquence may set fire to reason." On its surface, this part of the dissent looks questionable. The generally agreed-on difference between an expression of opinion and incitement is the difference between a speaker at a rally on Wall Street denouncing capitalism and the speaker yelling, "There's a hedge fund manager! Let's get him!" Incitement, as Nelles noted, speaks in the imperative. It is also one of the categories of speech that might currently be subject to punishment, yet Holmes seemed to be denying that any punishable speech existed. But Sanford did not use *incitement* in this general sense; he contrasted incitement to "philosophical abstraction," leaving nothing between the two. The "Left Wing Manifesto" was not "mere prediction," as Sanford accurately stated. It was Gitlow's hope that the American working class would follow the example of the Bolsheviks all the way to the Winter Palace. But it was not a call to immediate action, nor was it in any way likely to produce such action. So Sanford was using the term *incitement* in exactly the way Holmes described — "the speaker's enthusiasm for the result."

The next line contained the most dramatic and debatable sentence in the dissent: "If in the long run the beliefs expressed in proletarian dictatorship are destined to be accepted by the dominant forces of the community, the only meaning of free speech is that they should be given their chance and have their way." No other statement in a speech-rights case, before or since, has gone that far. In part, it is common sense decked out in Holmesian rhetorical style. If, in free and open debate, the ideas of the "Left Wing Manifesto" are accepted by popular majorities, then the people should get what they want, whether it is good for them or not. This was one of the speech-rights principles Holmes and Brandeis left for future Courts — that government cannot criminalize an idea for fear it might come to pass. It was basic to Holmes's constitutional view that if a democratic majority wants to go to hell in a handbasket, the Constitution does not prohibit it. But he is not quite clear here what the phrase "dominant forces" means. The sentence could be read to suggest that if a forceful and energetic minority becomes so committed to the insurrectionary preachings of the "Left Wing Manifesto" that its members "have their way" by undemocratic means, then so be it. This last possibility has led some critics to link Holmes's speech-rights doctrine to his occasional forays into social Darwinism.

Holmes's dissent does not rise or fall on that sentence, but even the more radical interpretation can be justified. Neither Holmes nor Brandeis (nor any subsequent justice) grounded his thinking on speech rights on the assumption that words have no consequences. Words suggesting awful deeds may in fact lead to awful outcomes. But that is the risk inherent in accepting the premises of free discussion. It is not a suicide pact; it is a considered judgment that the gains are worth the risks. More important, no specific long-term consequence is inevitable. Words and ideas are translated into behavior only after they are weighed against other inputs. And events in the years since the Court moved to accept the Holmes-Brandeis interpretation have provided a test. Gitlow-type agitation and other forms of advocacy that involve illegal means have generally been permitted in this country since the early 1930s. The movement toward overthrow of the constitutional order has been negligible. What *is* inevitable is that a speech-rights doctrine that allows legislatures, juries, and judges to decide which words might lead to future harm will wind up jailing Eugene Debs and Joseph Gilbert. That basic point united Holmes and Brandeis in spite of different emphases in their dissents and set them in opposition to the rest of the Court for almost the entire decade of the 1920s. Brandeis did more than sign the *Gitlow* dissent; he wrote "very good opinion, this" in a note to Holmes at the bottom of it.

The dissent has also been criticized for not directly addressing Sanford's contention that once the legislature has designated a specific doctrine as harmful, courts have no role in examining circumstances. First Amendment scholar Harry Kalven has argued that "Justices Holmes and Brandeis did not rise to the occasion. . . . Holmes ignored the distinction Justice Sanford had drawn between *Schenck* and the case at the bar." That is true; addressing that point was not among the "ten words" Holmes wanted to add to his previous thoughts. It would have been instructive if he had, because the only plausible conclusion he could have reached was the one Walter Pollak argued — that the law itself was unconstitutional, rather than its application being faulty. Holmes still shied away from overturning laws, as opposed to verdicts, perhaps a residue of the liberty-of-contract battles. Even his *Abrams* dissent did not question the constitutionality of the hideously repressive 1918 amendments to the Espionage Act. Here, the only response to Sanford would have been that the New York legislature had no constitutional right to do what it did.

This and other criticisms of Holmes's dissent in *Gitlow* are in large measure a product of its mix of brevity and passion. He and Brandeis were simply not on the same page as the Court majority. Their differences were not over fine points. Holmes and Brandeis had moved toward a view, expressed differently in different dissents, that speech could be judged criminal only if it were likely to result in immediate illegal acts. They thought there was something to be gained by allowing even the speech of someone like Gitlow, who opposed democratic government; the majority believed there was nothing to be lost by prohibiting it. The constitutional arguments proceeded from those opposed mind-sets. Sanford's motivating thought was this one: "Reasonably limited . . . this freedom [of speech] is an inestimable privilege in a free government; without such limitation, it might become the scourge of the republic." From that vantage point, tolerating the "Left Wing Manifesto" made no sense. Immediately after the ruling, Holmes wrote to Frederick Pollock that "the prevailing notion of free speech seems to be that you may say what you want if you don't shock *me*." Elsewhere he added, "Of course the value of the constitutional right is only when you do shock people." Holmes's explanation in the *Gitlow* dissent of his differences with "reasonably limited" speech was not his most complete. But the fact that the litigant was an aspiring American Bolshevik demonstrated the strength of Holmes's convictions.

Back in the World

By the time the Supreme Court decision was handed down, Ben Gitlow had been out on parole for more than two years and was heavily involved in Communist work. The party itself took very little interest in the case. Minutes of the party's Executive Committee meetings held right before and after the decision do not indicate that it was discussed at all. Ruthenberg in the *Daily Worker* did comment on it, calling the decision "a striking confirmation of the Communist contention that American democracy was a fraud." The *Worker* liked Holmes's line about beliefs in proletarian dictatorship "having their way," repeating it three times in editorials appearing over two days but demonstrating no understanding of what Holmes was actually saying. Gitlow later self-critically admitted that he saw the case as trivial compared to the other issues that held Communists' attention: "A fight in a local union of the needle trades that was far removed from the political life of the country assumed far greater importance than did this decision which so narrowed freedom of speech."

The practical effects could not be so easily ignored. In November, Gitlow was ordered to report back to Sing Sing. Once inside, he renewed old acquaintances: "I was greeted humorously as the man who goes in and out of jail at will." But he did not expect to stay long. On the day of the Supreme Court decision, the ACLU announced that it would be seeking a pardon. The case for a pardon was strong—Gitlow had served more than twice as long as Larkin and Winitsky and had diligently pursued every legal remedy available to him. Those who wrote letters to the governor on his behalf pointed to the two dissenters in the Supreme Court and the two in the court of appeals. The foreman of the jury that had convicted him wrote a letter calling for a pardon, emphasizing that the work of upholding New York law had been completed with the Supreme Court decision and that no further good would be served by keeping Gitlow in jail. But Governor Smith moved slowly, saying he would make no decision until Gitlow was once again incarcerated. Coincidentally or not, this also meant that the pardon would not be issued until after the fall elections.

One of Gitlow's assignments while out on parole was to assume editorial control of *Freiheit*, a Jewish newspaper largely run by the party. Gitlow knew almost no Yiddish and was not comfortable with the job, but it was there that he met his future wife, Badana Zeitlin. She was not yet a party member, a fact that "was considered by most of my associates an unpardonable breach of Bolshevik conduct." They married on December 10, 1924, and he described their bond through all the tempestuous events of his life as "a union which has been a source of great happiness and has enabled me to overcome the pressure and strain of nerve-wracking events."

Badana visited him several times in Sing Sing while the pardon talks were in progress. The ACLU notified her on December 7, 1925, that a pardon was forthcoming, "with the single reservation that a necessary delay may intervene." She was visiting her husband in Sing Sing on their first anniversary, December 10, 1925, when she was called to the warden's office and notified that the governor had issued the pardon. It seems unlikely that Smith intended the melodrama, and in fact, the pardon did not become effective until it was officially filed the next day. But Gitlow could not resist describing the end of the six-year story that began with his arrest as "like a moving picture climax to a prison scene, liberation coming at the darkest moment and on the very day of the first wedding anniversary."

Smith's pardon statement was short and emphasized fairness and proportionality rather than civil liberties. He pointed to the similarity of Gitlow's case to Larkin's, about which he had written extensively, and he noted that Gitlow had been in prison far longer than anyone else convicted in the criminal anarchy trials. He noted the dissents in the court of appeals and the Supreme Court, as well as the opinion of the appeals court majority that the penalty was too harsh. "I am satisfied that the ends of justice have been met and no additional punishment would act as a deterrent to those who preach an erroneous doctrine of government. That he was convicted and that he was in prison is sufficient." On December 11, Gitlow, wearing "a heavy, ugly prison overcoat," walked out of Sing Sing.

CHAPTER 7

Playing with the Devil's Rattle

Reaction to the *Gitlow* decision was subdued. On the Supreme Court, the battle lines over speech rights had been clear for several years, and the only new element here was confirmation that Justice Sanford sided with the majority against Holmes and Brandeis. He offered the concept of "reasonably limited speech rights," and the majority thought that a manifesto from an American Bolshevik was a reasonable place to limit them. A *New York Times* editorial applauded that decision: "Any constituted government is entitled to protect itself against overthrow by violence."

The verdict got a cooler reception from the legal community, although there was little surprise. The Columbia, Harvard, and Yale law reviews noted the decision with mild disfavor, focusing on Sanford's rejection of the "circumstances" argument. Civil libertarians had hoped the Court would be ready to adopt a more generous attitude toward speech rights. The *Columbia Law Review* noted that the *Gitlow* verdict put that hope to rest, at least temporarily: "It was acclaimed that the war restrictions on free speech would be confined to war and that there was no chance . . . that they would be applied generally. The present case shows this is not so." Rather than expanding the use of Holmes's "clear and present danger" test, Sanford had ruled that courts could not invoke any test at all if the legislature had already determined a set of ideas to be inherently dangerous. The snakes, fires, and revolutionary sparks in the language of this case were a full-throated defense of the bad tendency doctrine.

Little attention was paid to Holmes's dissent, which was seen as a restatement of views he and Brandeis had been expressing since *Abrams*. Likewise, these law reviews paid surprisingly little attention to Sanford's "we may and do assume" incorporation stipulation. The only observer who drew attention to the importance of the incorporation element was alarmed by it. Charles Warren in the *Harvard Law Review* wrote that this stipulation — announced in "one short sentence" — would inevitably pave the way for a dramatic extension of rights. Warren pointed out that this sentence contained no argument or reference to precedent and that it reversed fifty years of contrary Court decisions. He also asked whether consistency would not require the extension of the establishment clause to the states and, after that, the rest of the Bill of Rights. That direction made him uneasy; individual rights had been and should be "purely the concern of the State and its own people and in no wise subject to interference by the National Government."

Warren turned out to be right about the legacy of the *Gitlow* case. The assumption that the First Amendment applied to the states led to an expansion of rights so significant that a book on the subject was titled *The Second Bill of Rights*. Because most controversies involving rights are local, the incorporation aspect of *Gitlow* became its most important legacy. Of 117 citations of *Gitlow* in federal court decisions, 87 were for its role in extending the Bill of Rights to the states, and only 30 were for any substantive argument on speech rights.

The civil libertarians, in contrast, turned out to be wrong. The *Gitlow* decision was not the beginning of wider suppression of speech. Within a few years (and a few changes in Court personnel), Holmes's dissent rather than Sanford's majority opinion would become the Court consensus.

Gitlow's Fellow Travelers

The *Gitlow* majority opinion contained two rulings: that the First Amendment would be assumed to apply to the states (at least in this case), but it provided no protection for the speech of admitted revolutionaries. Both these themes were immediately reinforced in cases following *Gitlow*.

The first, *Ruthenberg v. Michigan*, shared enough DNA with the *Gitlow* case to be its cousin. The defendant, Charles E. Ruthenberg, had also been a defendant in the criminal anarchy trials. His codefendant in the New York case, Isaac E. Ferguson, was at his side again, but only as Ruthenberg's lawyer (having removed himself from Communist circles). The charge against Ruthenberg — that he had violated Michigan's criminal syndicalism law — went the New York charges one better: the crime was not advocating illegal means of change but assembling with others who did. He had been arrested at a gathering of Communists in Bridgman, Michigan, in August 1922. The meeting had been called under pressure from the Comintern to resolve factional disputes, and it was intended to be secret and the records of it buried. But one of the delegates was an informant for the Justice Department and helped coordinate a raid by the local police. Ruthenberg was charged with violating the Michigan law less than two months after the dismissal of his New York charges.

Ruthenberg, as his New York testimony had demonstrated, was completely open and candid about being a Communist leader. That admission and his presence at the meeting were enough for a Michigan jury to convict Ruthenberg and for the judge to sentence him to three to ten years. The appeal focused directly on the part of the criminal syndicalism law that made it a felony to assemble with other seditious people. The Michigan Supreme Court did not dispute the *Gitlow* stipulation that the Fourteenth Amendment extended First Amendment protection to the states. But it did make short work of the substantive argument. The defense argued that the Communist writings confiscated at Bridgman were merely "prophetic" of class conflict; the court's response was that "the naivety of this should make a Communist smile. . . . [T]hey are militant prophets, to say the least." It also offered its own vivid bad tendency metaphor, taken from a seventeenth-century English writer: "They which played with the devil's rattle will be brought by degrees to wield his sword."

The U.S. Supreme Court heard the case in April 1926, less than a year after the *Gitlow* decision. Ferguson referred to the incorporation of the First Amendment as a settled issue, despite Sanford's "For present purposes" stipulation. The lawyers for Michigan implicitly accepted that point. Only Brandeis seemed to show any buyer's remorse, in his case motivated by the freer hand it might give to the liberty-of-contract advocates on the Court. An early draft of his *Ruthenberg* opinion included an acknowledgment that expansion of the Fourteenth Amendment to include "matters of substantive law as well as procedure" was a settled issue. But that must not have sat well with him. In later versions of the opinion, he inserted a handwritten reservation — that the expansion had happened "despite arguments to the contrary." He strengthened that reservation even more in the final version: "despite arguments to the contrary *which had seemed to me persuasive*" (emphasis added). This was the final significant expression of doubt from any member of the Court about the Sanford stipulation, and it came, ironically, from one of the two justices who were most intent on broadening the protections of the First Amendment.

The Court's seven-to-two division in *Ruthenberg* was predictable — "*Gitlow v. New York* all over again," in the words of the two writers who have studied it most extensively. Brandeis attacked the bad tendency reasoning of the majority: "Every denunciation of existing law tends in some measure to increase the probability that there will be some violation of it." But the historical importance of the *Ruthenberg* dissent is his explanation of free speech as a prerequisite of democratic governance. "In a democracy public discussion is a duty," Brandeis wrote. "Those who won our independence by revolution [the inclusion of this word could not have been unintentional] valued liberty both as an end and as a means." And "the greatest menace to freedom is an inert people." This emphasis on the importance of the free exchange of ideas in democratic deliberation was somewhat different from what Holmes had written in *Abrams* and *Gitlow*. But Holmes signed the dissent, and there is no indication that he saw it as anything other than complementary to his own views.

Brandeis's dissent would have become an important part of the free-speech legacy he and Holmes created except for one unpredictable aspect of the case: on March 2, 1927, before the decision was made public, Charles Ruthenberg died. Ben Gitlow, after his pardon, had become a leading member of Ruthenberg's faction of the party and was a pallbearer at his funeral. Ruthenberg's unexpected death set off a new round of factional conflict and began a chain of events that would wind up with Gitlow's expulsion from the party (explained in the epilogue). It also mooted the case, leaving Brandeis with an opinion all dressed up and looking for a place to go.

Where that dissent (or large parts of it) came to rest was *Whitney v. California*. Anita Whitney, like Gitlow, was a Left Wing Socialist who joined the exodus that created the Communist Party. Though residing in California, she joined the same factional variant as Gitlow, the Communist Labor Party. And like Gitlow, she was arrested shortly after joining, more or less for the crime of being a prominent Communist. Her prominence came not from being a party leader but from being a member of a well-known family and the niece of former Supreme Court justice Stephen Field. Whitney was charged under California's criminal syndicalism law for her membership in an organization advocating violence. The evidence at her trial centered on the activities of the Industrial Workers of the World, much as Gitlow's case had focused on the Winnipeg strike. The prosecution's logic was that Whitney was a founding member of the Communist Labor Party, that her party had praised the IWW, and that the IWW advocated and in some cases even carried out industrial sabotage. That was enough for a conviction.

Whitney's case was argued in the Supreme Court on March 1926, but the decision was not released until April 1927, a month after Ruthenberg died. Significantly, there was no argument about the appropriateness of the Court hearing a speech-rights case based on state law. Brandeis repeated his "despite arguments to the contrary that I found persuasive" phrase from the unpublished *Ruthenberg* dissent (in fact, he repeated many parts of that unpublished opinion). But a subtle change indicated greater acceptance of Sanford's stipulation. In *Ruthenberg*, Brandeis had said that incorporation of the right to speech "*has been* settled"; here, he said it "*is* settled" (emphases added). The first made it seem as though something had been forced on him; the second put the issue beyond question. The debate about incorporation was over before it ever occurred.

Sanford wrote the majority opinion, and his arguments were largely a reiteration of *Gitlow*, without the snakes and smoldering fires. If the California law had a reasonable basis, it would get "every presumption" of constitutionality. There was "no absolute right to speak without responsibility." Brandeis, with Holmes joining, used the opportunity to make his *Ruthenberg* reasoning public. He repeated part of that dissent verbatim but added even more sweeping words about the value of free expression to democracy: "Those who won our independence by revolution were not cowards," and "Men feared witches and burnt women." But the overall point was the same: "Without free speech and assembly, discussion would be futile." Weighed against these values, speech could be punished only when it constituted incitement that "would be immediately acted on" — the point

Holmes had made in *Gitlow*. In this case, Brandeis found that Whitney's lawyers had not submitted any evidence disputing the state's charge of incitement, so his opinion was actually a concurrence that took issue with the majority's reasoning more thoroughly than most dissents.

The Court released two related decisions on the same day as *Whitney*. In one, *Burns v. United States*, the Court, by its familiar seven-to-two margin, upheld the conviction of William Burns for passing out IWW literature in Yosemite Park. The other, *Fiske v. Kansas*, pointed in a different direction. Harold Fiske, an IWW organizer, had been arrested for carrying recruiting material. He was convicted under the Kansas Criminal Syndicalism Act, with the sole evidence against him being the preamble to the IWW constitution: "The working class and the employing class have nothing in common. . . . Between these two classes a struggle must go on until the workers of the world organize as a class and take possession of the earth and the machinery of production and abolish the wage system." Sanford, writing for a unanimous Court, ruled that those words alone did not have the "sinister meaning" the prosecution gave them. Thus, Fiske had been convicted without evidence that a crime had been committed. Most recent analysts have argued that *Fiske* was not a speech-rights case at all. But it is not hard to imagine the Court construing the IWW preamble as evidence of illegal advocacy. The majority had been creative in finding a link between advocacy and illegal activity in *Gitlow* and even more so in *Whitney*, which rested on the language of the IWW. Fiske had testified that "the IWW expected to rule the world" and that, when it did, "all people would be equalized." By not concluding that those ends could be accomplished only through violent means—as it had in *Gitlow*—the Court appeared to be inching away, very slightly, from the most extreme versions of the bad tendency doctrine.

In the three cases decided that day, no objection was raised to the Court's invoking the First Amendment in reviewing state law. Both sides in the *Fiske* case mentioned the *Gitlow* "we may and do assume" stipulation as though it were accepted doctrine. On the scope of the protections provided by the First Amendment, the majority referred to *Gitlow* as its default position, although in *Fiske*, it signaled that the prosecution had to at least go through the motions of connecting words to illegal acts.

Red Flags and Red Orators

The next set of speech-rights cases demonstrated that the incorporation element of *Gitlow* had quickly become set in concrete and that, nearly as quickly, a majority on the Court was moving in the direction of the Holmes-Brandeis dissents. In part, this was due to a change in the composition of the Court. From the time of *Whitney*, *Burns*, and *Fiske*, Sanford and Chief Justice William Howard Taft were out; Charles Evans Hughes and Owen Roberts were in, and both new justices regularly voted for an expansion of speech rights. But personnel change was not the only factor. Harlan Stone, who had voted with the *Whitney* majority, began to side with Holmes, Brandeis, and the newer members in their interpretation of the First Amendment. George Sutherland and Willis Van Devanter, who had joined the *Gitlow* majority (and would become half of the Court conservatives who battled Roosevelt), also began to vote with the newly libertarian majority at times. It is not clear what led to the change by any of these three justices. Perhaps it was simply a product of the eloquence and logical force of the Holmes-Brandeis dissents. It was not a reflection of more peaceful times. The next set of cases arrived at the onset of the Depression, and those involving Communists were dealing with a party whose program and rhetoric had moved so far to the left after the late 1920s that Ben Gitlow himself had been expelled for being insufficiently revolutionary.

A sharp break with the *Gitlow* and *Whitney* decisions came in the next major speech-rights case. Yetta Stromberg, a nineteen-year-old member of the Young Communist League of California, was arrested after taking part in a Communist youth camp in 1929 with forty children and six other adults. Every morning, Stromberg raised a red flag and led the children in a "pledge of allegiance to the working class." She was convicted under California's "Red Flag Law," making it a crime to display any symbol of "opposition to organized government." Her appeal reached the Supreme Court in 1931.

California argued that *Gitlow* had settled all the questions in the case: the government has an inherent right of self-protection, and when it passed laws to that end, they deserved a very wide benefit of the doubt. The first sentence of the state's brief referred to the *Gitlow* verdict, and seven other *Gitlow* citations followed. The state did have to get creative, however, in applying the bad tendency test to an isolated camp for children at which a red flag was raised. Stromberg, it said, was "creating the spark in them which when fanned might burst into a great conflagration." That argument almost certainly would have been enough for the Court of 1925, and Pierce Butler expressed the old standard in dissent: anarchy "is certain to follow a successful opposition to organized government." But this time the Court majority rejected that approach and overturned Stromberg's conviction. Chief Justice Hughes focused on a single point—that one clause of the California law was too broad, and it was impossible to tell whether that clause had played a role in Stromberg's conviction. But the Court was launched in a new direction. Although Hughes did not try to match the earlier rhetorical flourishes of Holmes and Brandeis (who voted with him), he put this case in the framework they had created: "The maintenance of the opportunity for free political discussion to the end that government may be responsive to the will of the people . . . is a fundamental principle of our constitutional system."

The incorporation aspect of *Stromberg* was notable for its absence, not its presence. Neither side argued the point, and the dissenters did not mention it. In *Near v. Minnesota*, decided two weeks after *Stromberg*, the extent of the incorporation doctrine was reargued one more time. *Near* concerned the use of a public nuisance law in Minnesota to close down a scandalmongering newspaper. The state argued that the Court had never formally accepted the incorporation of the First Amendment and that even Sanford's conditional endorsement in *Gitlow* had not mentioned the "free press" clause. The brief mentioned Warren's article describing the negative consequences of going down the path of incorporation. Hughes responded emphatically to that issue in his majority opinion overturning the Minnesota law: "It is no longer open to doubt that the liberty of the press and of speech is safeguarded by the due process clause of the 14th Amendment from invasion by state action." Butler, writing in dissent, noted that although he had misgivings about incorporation, *Gitlow* had been the watershed moment. It was. Following the exchange in *Near*, the Court argued over when, how, and even why to incorporate other parts of the Bill of Rights, but it never again questioned the *Gitlow* precedent.

When the Court returned to Communism, it became clear how far the free-speech goalposts had been moved. The Court overturned the convictions of the next two Communist defendants whose cases came before it. Although the majority worked to tailor an opinion to the particulars of each case, there is little question that the *Gitlow* or *Whitney* majority would have upheld the convictions. The first case involved Dirk De Jonge, a Communist leader in Portland, Oregon, who was arrested during a bitter dock strike in 1934. Following the shooting of four strikers, the Communist Party organized a protest meeting with about 300 participants. De Jonge addressed the crowd openly as a party member and urged people both to join the party and to "come to a rally the next day in defiance of the police." He was convicted for organizing and speaking at a meeting advocating criminal anarchy.

In *De Jonge v. Oregon*, the Court set aside the conviction. The state relied heavily on the *Gitlow* ruling, including in its brief a lengthy quotation from Sanford's "a single revolutionary spark may kindle a fire" explanation of the bad tendency doctrine. De Jonge's lawyers differentiated the two cases: there was no manifesto with De Jonge's name on it, and his speech had not advocated anything illegal. They attacked Sanford's theory that a legislative determination of which doctrines are inherently dangerous eliminated the courts' role in examining circumstances: "Many laws have been declared void despite express legislative declaration of their necessity." The unanimous verdict, like the defense brief, emphasized the specifics — this was a peaceful assembly conducted by a political party that had been on the ballot in Oregon in 1932. The decision sidestepped any criticism of *Gitlow* by pointing to factual differences. But it could have noted the similarities just as easily. De Jonge, like Gitlow, did not hide his Communist affiliation. De Jonge's speech might not have advocated the overthrow of the government, but other local party literature did. Whereas Gitlow had been convicted in part because of a fleeting reference to a strike in Canada, De Jonge advocated class warfare in the middle of a violent strike in Portland. It was not the particulars of the cases that were different; it was the Court's view of speech rights.

The case following on the heels of *De Jonge* shared some of its features, but there was one significant difference: although the defendant was a Communist, he was also an African American. Angelo Herndon helped organize a rally in Atlanta, Georgia, to publicize the existence of hunger during the Depression. There were no illegal acts at the rally, nor did the leaflets passed out at the rally call for any. But Herndon was charged under a Georgia pre–Civil War anti-insurrection law. Like De Jonge, his Communist affiliation and the party's literature were central to the evidence against him. The state emphasized a pamphlet outlining the party's somewhat bizarre call for "self-determination in the Black Belt," based on the supposition that African Americans constituted a nation in those contiguous areas of the South where they formed a majority and that they had the right to secede. The Black Belt theory had been foisted on the party by the Communist International and was largely ignored in practice. But it caught the eye of the Georgia prosecutors as being especially inflammatory.

The Supreme Court got the case six months after *De Jonge*, and again, much of the state's case focused on *Gitlow*. The state argued that, based on *Gitlow*, it was sufficient to establish that a person or publication created a "dangerous tendency," and no showing of a "clear and present danger" was necessary. The Court, by the thinnest of margins, rejected that approach. For the majority, Roberts wrote that speculation about future effects would "license the jury to create its own standards." In response to the lesson Georgia drew from *Gitlow*, he added: "the power of the state to abridge freedom of speech and assembly is the exception rather than the rule." The four conservative justices dissented, citing Sanford's "kill the snake when it is young" logic. Why the dissent in *Herndon* and not in *De Jonge*? Van Devanter provided a clue in the dissent: "It should not be overlooked that Herndon was [a] negro member and organizer in the Communist Party." The four dissenters mentioned the Black Belt theory as an example of the magnitude of the "dangerous tendency" in this case.

Bound up with the change of outcomes in these speech cases was an upgrade in the status of the Holmes-Brandeis dissents of the 1920s. Briefs for defendants started to refer to those dissents as though they represented the voice of the Court as early as *Near v. Minnesota*, the last major speech case decided while both Holmes and Brandeis were still on the Court. Briefs for both *De Jonge* and *Herndon* drew from Brandeis's opinion in *Whitney*. That was strategically wise; since Brandeis's opinion was formally a concurrence, the lawyers could, with a little sleight of hand, transform it into the opinion of the Court. More daringly, the brief for *Herndon* contained a long extract from Holmes's "time has upset many fighting faiths" dissent in *Abrams*. The defendants, of course, had every reason to prefer the reasoning in these dissents to the majority opinions. But there was no apology for citing the dissents, implying that the lawyers must have known the new Court majority looked on them favorably.

By the late 1930s the Court itself began citing the Holmes-Brandeis dissents regularly, as though they, not the majority opinions, should be seen as precedents. In *U.S. v. Carolene Products*, Stone cited Holmes's *Gitlow* opinion as though it were the received wisdom of the Court in the area of "interference with political organization." In another Communist case (*Bridges v. California*), Hugo Black mentioned the *Abrams* and *Gitlow* dissents and the *Whitney* concurrence as precedents. In *Thomas v. Collins* (1945), the Court overturned the conviction of a United Automobile Workers leader for failing to register with the state when speaking about unionization in Texas. Writing for the Court, Wiley Rutledge twice mentioned the *Abrams* and *Gitlow* dissents, drawing from them the lesson that "free trade in ideas means free trade in the opportunity to persuade to action, not merely to describe facts." What is notable about this transformation is not merely that the Court began to adopt the two dissenters' reasoning but also that it dispensed with any argument about whether the dissents rather than the actual rulings should be regarded as precedents.

So Yetta Stromberg, Dirk De Jonge, and Angelo Herndon went free after doing more or less the same thing Ben Gitlow had done in 1919. Harry Bridges, a Communist longshoremen's union leader, had his deportation order overturned by the Supreme Court, as did another Communist leader, William Schneiderman.

A contempt conviction for Bridges — for threatening to strike if a court decision went against his union — was also reversed. Black, speaking for a unanimous Court in the contempt case, summarized the new consensus: "the substantive evil must be extremely serious, and the degree of imminence extremely high, before utterances can be punished."

Bad Tendency, Back from the Ashes

That consensus changed following World War II. The end of the war segued almost immediately into the Cold War, with the Communist

Party of the United States now supporting the goals of America's adversary. The party had disbanded during the wartime alliance between the United States and the Soviet Union, but with an unsubtle push from Moscow, the party expelled its leader, Earl Browder, and reconstituted itself immediately after the war. There were also several extremely high-profile revelations and trials involving party-linked espionage. In the highest ranks of the FBI and the intelligence community, the secret decoding of cable traffic (the Venona Project) revealed that spying was more prevalent than even the sensational allegations suggested and that the party organized and directed that activity. Although none of these external circumstances had any direct relationship to First Amendment issues, they created an environment that could not help but influence both the public and the courts. Although the Venona Project was so secret that even President Truman did not know about it, and the intelligence obtained could not be used in court to substantiate espionage claims, it provided a great incentive for those with access to this information to pursue party leaders on whatever grounds were available. This helps explain why the government's spying cases generally look better in hindsight, and its political prosecutions look worse. To pursue the latter, the government had to dust off the bad tendency doctrine and the "inherent right of self-protection" argument from the 1920s, which had fallen into disfavor.

The extremity of the evil was the government's building block in most of these cases. In *American Communications Association v. Douds*, the Court upheld the section of the Taft-Hartley Act requiring union leaders to take anti-Communist oaths as the price of access to the National Labor Relations Board. To the dissenting Black, this was an uncomplicated First Amendment case. To the majority, it was not about speech rights at all. After clearing their throats with a few words of praise for the Holmes-Brandeis dissents, the majority found a way around the First Amendment by comparing the issues in *Douds* to the Court's approval of the internment of Japanese Americans during World War II. Communist union leaders were "like termites undermining American industry," intending to cripple it with political strikes. Free speech was not the question; this case was about the "free flow of commerce."

But a direct confrontation between the First Amendment and national security could not be put off for long. It came the year after

Douds, and *Gitlow v. New York* was a featured player. Eugene Dennis, who had replaced Browder as general secretary of the Communist Party, and ten other party leaders were charged with conspiring to overthrow the U.S. government by force and violence, in violation of the Smith Act of 1940. The charges, and the evidence presented at trial, drew from the general body of Marxist-Leninist literature and party material, not from specific instances of direct criminal advocacy. The prosecution argued that the literature contained goals that could be achieved only through force and that the defendants advocated such ends. It made no difference that the goals were implausible; it only mattered that these leaders were intent on bringing them into being as soon as practicable. In short, save for the Cold War context, this was *Gitlow* redux. As with the original, conviction was a foregone conclusion.

The Supreme Court upheld the convictions, by a vote of six to two. The defense drew a direct comparison to *Gitlow*, aware that Holmes's dissent had come to be viewed as the real precedent: "Ultimately, all of the justifications for this statute [the Smith Act] and its applications lead back to the *Gitlow* case." The brief traced the transformation of Court references to the original *Gitlow* verdict through the cases of the 1930s. "In none of [these cases] was the *Gitlow* doctrine of bad tendency resorted to." Instead, "the principles developed by justices Holmes and Brandeis were assumed to be law." The brief summarized the legacy of the dissent this way: "If the body of constitutional adjudication which this Court has created in the past twenty-five years means anything, it means a rejection of the *Gitlow* case. . . . The case has become a symbol of the rejected view of the First Amendment."

The government pointed out that *Gitlow* (and *Whitney*) had never been explicitly overruled, and it claimed that the majority's logic in that case was sound. If the *Gitlow* rule were still in effect, no showing of clear and present danger would be necessary. Congress had found "serious danger to important national interests from a proscribed class of utterances which are inherently evil." With that done, "the First Amendment does not require the application of an additional test."

Just in case the Court would not accept the "legislative determination" argument from *Gitlow*, the government also described plenty of danger and argued that it was quite clear. These Communist defendants were "American leaders of a world wide totalitarian political movement" that was secretive, tightly disciplined, and prepared to "employ fully the method of military aggression, civil war, espionage, sabotage, and mendacious propaganda." As for the danger being "present," the government cited the overthrow of democracy in Czechoslovakia at the time of the defendants' arrests. It concluded by restating the essence of the case against these defendants in some of the same terms it had used to convict Gitlow: "the existence of specific intent to bring about the evils . . . increases the likelihood or probability that they will occur." So, kill the snake when it is young.

The Court majority acknowledged the centrality of *Gitlow* to both sides and handled the issue with kid gloves. In a concurrence, Frankfurter agreed with the defense's contention that the Court no longer regarded the majority holding as a precedent. "It would be disingenuous to deny that the dissent in *Gitlow* has been treated with the respect usually accorded to a decision." A lower court had argued that the *Gitlow* decision remained good law; the majority in *Dennis* did not go that far. It tried to walk a tightrope, praising Holmes while denying that his reasoning applied in this case. Robert Jackson wrote in another concurrence, "The names Holmes and Brandeis cannot be associated with such a doctrine of governmental disability [lacking the power to punish a conspiracy]." Why not? Because, as Frederick Vinson wrote for the Court, "The situation with which Justices Holmes and Brandeis were concerned in *Gitlow* was a comparatively isolated event, bearing little relation in their minds to any substantial threat to the safety of the community." Frankfurter tried to distinguish the cases by soft-pedaling the facts of *Gitlow*: Ben Gitlow was a "left wing Socialist" who published a "Manifesto expressing Marxist exhortation."

None of this was true, nor is it what Holmes believed at the time. These rationalizations may have convinced the majority that it was not dishonoring Holmes, but they were not accurate. Gitlow was not a street-corner prophet or an isolated leftist crank. The "Left Wing Manifesto" was a call to create an American Bolshevik-style party with a program of taking power (eventually) through insurrection. The manifesto was more forthright about that goal than the *Dennis* defendants had been. None of them came close to making the kind of "I am a revolutionist" speech to the jury that Gitlow had. At the time of the criminal anarchy trials, there were more Communists (in the several parties together) than there were members of the Communist Party of the United States in 1951. Although there was no Cold War in 1919, the Bolshevik revolution had just taken place, and there was a real fear that it would be repeated elsewhere. Anarchist bombings had occurred in New York and Washington several months before Gitlow's arrest. That could hardly have escaped Holmes's notice — he was a target of one of the bombs.

With obeisance paid to Holmes, the Court now walked away from the point of his dissents. In his concurrence, Frankfurter leaned on legislative determination and its heavy presumption of constitutionality. That had been a central point for Sanford, but it was also a common one for Frankfurter. Here, he simply noted that First Amendment cases were not an exception to that presumption. Vinson, writing for the Court majority, adopted as a test the phrase "the gravity of the evil discounted by its improbability," formulated by Judge Learned Hand in sustaining the convictions. That was the new version of "clear and present danger." If the danger was clear enough and evil enough, its presentness was not an issue. The government's arguments had dealt extensively with fifth column activity (that is, domestic support for Soviet goals), espionage, and sabotage. Sanford had not used "the gravity of the evil" phraseology, but in every step of the case against Gitlow, beginning with William McAdoo's police court, prosecutors and judges had outlined the goals of the "Left Wing Manifesto" and society's stake in preventing them. The gravity of the evil was exactly what Holmes was referring to in his controversial line about proletarian dictatorship being given its way if brought about by free expression. To Holmes, free speech was no less a constitutional obligation if it might be used to achieve bad ends.

Dennis left a complicated, almost schizophrenic legacy for *Gitlow*'s standing as a precedent. On the one hand, it all but announced that Holmes's dissent in *Gitlow*, not the majority opinion, would be regarded as binding precedent. On the other hand, the majority ruled that application of that precedent *upheld* the *Dennis* convictions, in spite of the similarities of the two cases. That reasoning had implications for the continued use of the New York criminal anarchy law. In 1964 New York prosecutors charged Bill Epton, an African American member of the Progressive Labor Party, with criminal anarchy (among other things) in connection with the Harlem riots that year. Epton had spoken at a meeting to protest the killing of a black teenager by the police. He said, "They [the police] declared war on us and we should declare war on them and every time they kill one of us damn it, we'll kill one of them." In private meetings Epton also suggested luring the police onto side streets in order to attack them and instructed followers in the use of Molotov cocktails. He was convicted of criminal anarchy as well as conspiracy to riot. The New York Court of Appeals agreed that the criminal anarchy law, as written in 1902 and interpreted in 1919, was unconstitutional. But it also said that the government was entitled to interpret the law in light of *Dennis* — that an intent to accomplish the violent acts had to be demonstrated, and that a court could affirm the existence of a "clear and present danger" based on circumstances. Limited in this way, the constitutionality of the criminal anarchy law was affirmed. The U.S. Supreme Court refused to hear the case because the one-year sentence for conspiracy to riot — which was not seriously contested — and the sentence for criminal anarchy were concurrent, eliminating the need to address the First Amendment question. So the criminal anarchy law had survived its brush with Holmes's dissent.

Justices Thunder Condemnation

Within a few years of the *Dennis* decision, prosecutions of Communists began to diminish as the domestic Communism issue burned itself out. The Court also began to find reasons to overturn some of the convictions. It offered somewhat far-fetched rationales for differentiating later cases from earlier ones. This was most notable in *Yates v. United States*, where the Court said that abstract advocacy of political violence was not enough to sustain a conviction. In reality, the Court was confirming Black's prediction in his *Dennis* dissent — that "in calmer times, when present pressures, passions, and fears subside," the Supreme Court would return to its pre-1950 First Amendment consensus.

One of the cases, *Noto v. United States*, produced a ruling that pointed toward a resolution of the sedition question raised in *Gitlow* and redebated through *Dennis*. John Francis Noto was convicted in 1954 on the same grounds as the *Dennis* defendants — that he had conspired to create political change by violent means. He was a Communist Party leader in New York State, a position roughly parallel to Harry Winitsky's in the criminal anarchy trials. The Court reversed Noto's conviction on the grounds that the prosecution had failed to prove that he personally advocated the overthrow of the government, even though his party did. The decision raised a more general point that, properly understood, would undermine the arguments of the *Gitlow* and *Dennis* majorities: "The mere abstract teaching of Communist theory, including the theory of the moral propriety or even moral necessity for a resort to force and violence, is not the same as preparing a group for violent action and steeling it to such action."

The heart of the prosecution of Ben Gitlow had been that he did not merely predict that violent political conflict would occur; he wanted it to occur, urged it along, and tried to convince others that it should. That was advocacy of illegality. The *Noto* verdict changed that. Maintaining that violence was a "moral necessity" — which Gitlow certainly did in 1919 — would no longer be sufficient to demonstrate illegal advocacy. The language in *Noto* on "preparing" and "steeling" shortened the chain-link causality of bad tendency and had the potential to expand speech protection significantly.

That expansion took place in *Brandenburg v. Ohio*, and again, *Gitlow* and the Holmes dissent played a role. Clarence Brandenburg was a Ku Klux Klan leader who invited TV reporters to film a rally at which hooded Klansmen marched, some of them holding weapons. One of the speakers said that if the government continued to suppress the white race, there might have to be "revengeance" taken; another said, "I believe the nigger should be returned to Africa, the Jew returned to Israel." Brandenburg was convicted under Ohio's criminal syndicalism law for advocating violence or terrorism as a means of political change.

Lawyers for the state argued before the Supreme Court that Ohio's law was no different in any important way from New York's criminal anarchy law, California's criminal syndicalism law (at issue in *Whitney*), and the Smith Act. The Court had upheld convictions based on all three. To make it clear that it was not running away from these precedents, the state's brief quoted from Sanford's opinion in *Gitlow* on the presumed validity of a legislative judgment about dangerous doctrines. The defense, for its part, repeated the losing argument of *Dennis* — that upholding the conviction would be "to turn away from the constitutional precepts enunciated by justices Holmes and Brandeis." The emphasis on these precedents meant that if the Court wanted to, it could bring some resolution to a sixty-year conflict over speech rights.

It did. Rather than bob and weave away from the precedents the two sides put on the table, the Court addressed them definitively and created a consensus that has lasted, with remarkably little division. Although the Holmes and Brandeis dissents are most noted for their eloquence on the value of free expression, they also contain a decision-making rule: speech can be prohibited only when the consequences are illegal, very serious, and imminent. The last word is the important one. A speaker cannot be punished because of words that might cause someone in the future to engage in illegality; he or she must incite illegality that is likely to happen here and now. The *Brandenburg* ruling skipped the eloquence and went right to the "imminence" rule, adopting it, strengthening it, and adding the requirement that the illegality must be probable as well as imminent. In overturning Brandenburg's conviction, the Court ruled that speech is criminal only when it is "directed to inciting imminent lawless action and is likely to incite or produce such action." By borrowing the "steeling" language from *Noto*, it made the requirement of direct incitement even more stringent. Black added in concurrence that this new standard would replace the mushier "clear and present danger" test, under which the Court had intermittently upheld convictions from *Schenck* to *Dennis*. *Brandenburg* did not create an absolute protection for speech. It did not say, as it could have, that only those who actually commit illegal acts or conspire with others to do so should be punished. But in practice, it has been extraordinarily difficult to get a conviction upheld for speech alone under an "imminent lawless action" test. Antiwar and leftist agitation in the late 1960s and early 1970s surpassed in tone anything Debs or Gitlow wrote, but there was little attempt to employ antisedition laws against it (and even less success). There may be some softening around the edges of the *Brandenburg* consensus in national security cases (as there often is), but as of now, reliance on the test articulated in that case unites most liberals and conservatives on the Court.

There is little doubt that, under the *Brandenburg* rule, all the famous convictions in the 1920s speech cases would be reversed. Mark Graber has argued that *Gitlow* would be the closest call, but this does not seem plausible. The *Brandenburg* Court would likely agree with Walter Nelles's argument in the *Gitlow* appeal that "incitement speaks in the imperative." There was nothing imperative in the ponderous language of the "Left Wing Manifesto." As Isaac E. Ferguson argued in his own criminal anarchy case, there was no specific set of hearers to incite. The prosecution at every level admitted that it did not expect any overt illegal acts to result from the manifesto, and Sanford stipulated his agreement with that. Ben Gitlow wanted to create a Leninist party in the United States to lead to the abolition of capitalism, and the manifesto explained that position in a tedious polemic. This was a far cry from the *Brandenburg* scenario of a speaker exhorting followers to immediate illegal acts that have a high likelihood of occurring.

The *Brandenburg* verdict overturned *Whitney* but not *Gitlow*, perhaps because the Court believed that the language of the *Dennis* majority had already accomplished that. Certainly, it contained no support for the bad tendency logic of the *Gitlow* majority. But lawyers and judges may note in the future that *Gitlow* was never explicitly overturned. The bad tendency principle, however battered, will not go away. It is not a foolish or malicious argument, which is why it reappears so frequently. It often seems to be the epitome of common sense. Holmes, in his *Abrams* dissent, pointed out that when most people are faced with a result they detest, their natural reaction is not to award rights to the advocates of that result but to try to stop or limit their advocacy. Sometimes lawless principles do increase the probability of lawless action. The "Left Wing Manifesto" did help create a Communist Party. Eugene Debs's praise for draft resisters might not have had much immediate effect, but it is possible that by becoming part of American history, it influenced draft resisters in the Vietnam era. The snake might simply have taken fifty years to strike.

Any new invocation of the bad tendency doctrine will have to go back to *Gitlow* and argue that the majority, not Holmes, was right. For instance, contemporary advocates of restrictions on "hate speech" generally believe that words of hate based on race, gender, and some other characteristics lead to discrimination and violence. To be consistent, they would have to support Sanford and his "reasonably limited" speech-rights argument. One such advocate, Alexander Tsesis, has taken up that challenge and written in support of Sanford: "The *Gitlow* majority thus clearly recognized the potentially long-term inflammatory effects of speech and understood the dangers of not immediately curbing instigatory words." Holmes, in this view, was irresponsibly cavalier about the possibility of "proletarian dictatorship" resulting from his free-speech principles. But Holmes was not arguing that words have no consequences. If anything, his starting point was the opposite one — that words have such important consequences that they should not be prohibited unless they are intended and likely to create illegal acts that are immediate and grave. He made that argument more dramatic by invoking worst-case scenarios: "freedom for the thought you hate and believe to be fraught with death" or, in the cases discussed here, words that advocate an end to democracy. What he and Brandeis shared in their dissents was a deep aversion to the only alternative: permitting government to be the arbiter of which ideas are considered useful and excluding the useless or harmful ones by coercion.

Holmes's dissent had another critic: Ben Gitlow. In *I Confess*, Gitlow addressed his case in a short paragraph and mentioned the two dissenters favorably, but without addressing the substance of what they said. In his later anti-Communist years, he implied that the majority had actually been right. He confided to his son in a lighthearted, confessional moment: "Of course I was guilty of what they charged me with — conspiring to overthrow the government." The implication, as Ben Jr. understood it, was that his father had successfully hidden his real purposes from his defenders at the time. That was how Ben Sr. saw the *Dennis* defendants and why he supported their convictions. But he was wrong. The civil libertarians of that period — Recht, Nelles, Pollak, Holmes, Brandeis, and Smith — were not gullible. They understood Gitlow's real intentions and what they were defending. But calling on American workers to follow the example of the Bolsheviks — or the Winnipeg strikers — was not the same as inciting or engaging in overt illegal acts to that end. They knew that the Ben Gitlow of 1919 was not a reform-minded dreamer, but they believed that the greater purposes of democracy were best served by permitting citizens to read the "Left Wing Manifesto," compare it with other information, and then decide for themselves whether to head for the barricades.

Epilogue

Most of the defendants in the famous Communist cases of the 1920s and 1930s moved on to lives with few dramatic twists. Anita Whitney and Dirk De Jonge remained lifelong prominent Communist Party members. Whitney became an iconic, almost legendary party figure, and at age eighty-two she was carried to a rally of longshoremen to speak against the Smith Act prosecutions. De Jonge was subpoenaed to testify in front of the House Un-American Activities Committee in 1956 and took the Fifth Amendment. Yetta Stromberg was active in liberal and leftist causes until her death at age ninety in 2008. She became a teacher, but because of the notoriety of her case, she was unable to teach in public schools. Angelo Herndon quietly left the party at the end of World War II, became a salesman, and played no further public role. He turned down requests to speak about his case. Each of the defendants led an eventful but reasonably predictable after-case life, either staying in the left-hand lane or bearing slightly right.

Gitlow's life, in contrast, resembled a tilt-a-whirl attached to a roller coaster. Immediately after the pardon he took a victory lap, beginning with a hero's reception in Grand Central Station that led to this reflection in his autobiography: "Little did I dream when the thunder of applause and cheering greeted the conclusion of my speech that the same movement that was cheering me so wildly, that movement that I helped build, would in the short order of ten years end by ostracizing me."

He enthusiastically threw himself back into party work, his standing boosted by the new prestige his case had generated. He ran for vice president on the Communist ticket in 1924 and 1928, helped oversee the party's labor work, and was on the board of the American Fund for Public Service, which funded liberal and leftist projects.

These efforts had modest results: the vote for the Communist ticket peaked at 48,000 in 1928, fewer votes than Socialist Party candidate Norman Thomas drew in New York City alone. But Gitlow's main activity was the same as that of other party leaders – dealing with the relentless internal party conflict, which was becoming increasingly intertwined with Stalin's ascension in the Soviet Union. Gitlow was a leader in the faction headed by Charles Ruthenberg and Jay Lovestone. In the mid-1920s the Comintern chose Ruthenberg's group to take over party leadership, and Gitlow's role grew after Ruthenberg's unexpected death and Lovestone's promotion. Gitlow went to Moscow in 1927 and 1928 and established a political and personal bond with Comintern chairman Nikolai Bukharin (as had Lovestone). When Stalin turned against Bukharin as the last obstacle to his consolidation of power, the Lovestone-Gitlow leadership became suspect, even though it had been elected by American party members. Communications from the Comintern to the American leadership were becoming increasingly worrisome. Lovestone decided to meet the troubling developments head-on, and in the spring of 1929 he and Gitlow led a delegation to Moscow to present its views to a specially created American Commission of the Comintern. To emphasize the importance of this meeting, Stalin attended personally.

That was the backdrop for what became a direct confrontation between Gitlow and Stalin. Members of the Lovestone group quickly realized that their closeness to Bukharin made them Stalin's targets and that they were in Moscow for an inquisition, not an adjudication. It became clear that, at the very least, Lovestone, Gitlow, and their associates would be stripped of their leadership roles. But they surprised Stalin by resisting that decision. Gitlow wrote to his wife, Badana, "We will not accept anything that is handed to us. While Hari-Kari may be heroic and a good method for old generals, we are yet young and our general principles do not include suicide." When the decision to remove them from leadership was formalized, the Americans were asked to state publicly whether they would support the decision. Most of the delegation, including Lovestone, said that although they would not oppose the decision, they reserved the right to disagree. That was bad enough (from Stalin's perspective). But Gitlow went further: "I cannot accept the demand made upon me here. . . . Not only do I vote against the decision, but when I return to the

United States I will fight against it." Stalin flew into a rage: "Trotsky defied me. Where is he? Bukharin defied me. Where is he? And you, who are you?"

Gitlow had spent his whole life in the revolutionary movement, including nearly three years in prison on its behalf. He respected the Russian revolutionaries but saw them as no more than Russian versions of himself. Even more, he did not think they had any special insight into American conditions. To accept a resolution condemning himself as a "Hooverite" — which is what he was being asked to do — would have been humiliating. In his final letter to Badana before leaving Moscow, he wrote, "I adopted the only course that one with respect for himself and some honesty could adopt. The strain of the fight here has been terrific. . . . But I am so glad I stood up." Gitlow, Lovestone, and others in their group were expelled from the party when they got back to the United States. As a final indignity, Gitlow's mother, Kate, was badgered to repudiate her son, and when she did not, she was expelled.

Gitlow's expulsion left him in a peculiar kind of limbo. Still a believer, he had been excommunicated from his secular church and was now a Leninist without a party. He, Lovestone, and about 200 others formed an organization called the Communist Party (Majority Group), claiming to be the "real" party because they were the elected leadership. But it was the Comintern that bestowed legitimacy, and this effort went nowhere. In 1933 Gitlow parted company with Lovestone because he felt that Lovestone was not sufficiently critical of Stalin. Gitlow was now convinced that Stalin was leading the Soviet Union down a terrible path, although he described it as a deviation from Lenin. He later formed two even smaller groups. Finally he rejoined the Socialist Party in 1935 — the party he had left with great fanfare in 1919, leading to the "Left Wing Manifesto."

Then in 1936 he went silent. Gitlow had always been a very public figure, writing speeches, pamphlets, and political letters nearly every month of his life. But there are few records from the year he began the decisive break with his past. Several factors led to his conversion. Gitlow's mini-parties had all been obvious failures, and the Socialists did not welcome him back enthusiastically. He was also persuaded that the stories drifting back from the Spanish Civil War about Stalin ordering his supporters to attack other leftists were true. But what hit

Gitlow hardest was the Great Purge in the Soviet Union—the show trials of former Bolshevik leaders. He followed these very closely, as evidenced by a large file of *New York Times* clippings about the trials among his papers. The purge was something he could understand through the lens of his own experience in Moscow in 1929. Gitlow was not disposed to accept any of the rationalizations his former associates (including Lovestone) offered, and he told Badana that he needed to publicly repudiate his Communist past. She told him that if he did, she would leave him. There was no political disagreement between husband and wife; Badana simply did not want to go through the controversies that were bound to follow a public announcement of his new views.

Her attitude changed in 1938 with the trial and immediate execution of Bukharin, with whom Gitlow had formed a brief but warm personal bond. In subsequent years, when he wrote vituperative attacks on every other foreign and domestic Communist, he never said a negative word about Bukharin. Both Gitlows now agreed; the situation demanded that Ben assume a new public role as an anti-Communist. The first step was his autobiography, which he had begun writing in 1937. The title *I Confess* was intended to mock the obviously staged "confessions" of those being executed in the Soviet purge. Successive drafts of the book demonstrate the rapid evolution of Gitlow's thinking, which was moving rightward almost month by month. In the first draft, Gitlow told about meeting Stalin for the first time and described the Russian leader as an ignoramus who "reminded me of Silent Cal Coolidge." His editor penciled in, "only less intelligent." In the final version, Gitlow accepted his editor's suggestion and added, "and far less decent"—now understanding that his new views would require a reinterpretation of his old ones.

The autobiography was close to publication when news broke of the Soviet-German nonaggression treaty. Gitlow managed to add only a brief mention of it on the book's final page. But the treaty led directly to the second step he took in his new role—testimony before the House Un-American Activities Committee in September 1939. He was there under subpoena, but he told the committee that before the Stalin-Hitler pact, "in all probability" he would have refused to testify. Now, however, he testified about the party's leadership structure by name, and he admitted that leaders—including himself—had smuggled precious jewels into the country to help finance the party in its early days. He also turned over a massive number of cables and other internal documents, which the editor of *I Confess* had used to verify many of the factual claims in the book. Gitlow's manner during the testimony was measured, and several times he tried to temper the more rabid committee investigators and members. At this point, he was still generally liberal in his political views. He was strongly supportive of labor and generally positive about Roosevelt. Under friendly questioning from Jerold Voorhis, the one liberal on the committee, he described himself as "the same as I ever was" on issues other than Communism. "There are many things in America that we have to apply ourselves to bring about a more equitable situation for the great masses of people of our country."

With the end of World War II and the beginning of the Cold War, Gitlow's political views drifted further right. Anti-Communism became the totality of his political world, and he aligned himself exclusively with conservatives. In the late 1930s he had cosponsored an event celebrating the life of anarchist Carlo Tresca, put on largely by left-wing anti-Stalinists. Following the war, Gitlow separated himself completely from that political company. He gave testimony helpful to the government's attempt to deport an economist named Lewis Corey—in reality, Gitlow's former Communist associate Louis Fraina, who was now an anti-Communist but still vaguely leftish. Gitlow wrote a scathing marginal commentary on a *New York Times Magazine* article by Sidney Hooks, putting a question mark next to Hooks's proposal for a broad anti-Communist movement uniting liberals and Socialists with conservatives and accusing Hooks of being insufficiently anti-Communist. He wrote a letter suggesting that Socialist Party leader Norman Thomas was covertly pro-Communist, and he joined the conservative attacks on Dwight Eisenhower for accepting the basic elements of the containment policy toward the Soviet Union. The most visible event he helped organize was a staged "Communist coup" in Mosinee, Wisconsin. Gitlow, as the new "commissar," ordered town residents marched to detention camps and decreed that restaurants could serve only black bread and potato soup. The Mosinee mayor, who cooperated with the performance, had a heart attack and died the next day, discouraging any more pseudo-coups.

Through all these activities, Gitlow had to make a living. At first, he was paid fifty dollars a session as a professional anti-Communist witness and similar amounts as a speaker, but those opportunities dwindled as the Cold War stabilized and the passions around domestic Communism cooled. He wrote letters to Herbert Hoover, J. Edgar Hoover, and Richard Nixon seeking employment as an expert on Communism but was politely rebuffed. By the 1950s Gitlow had a great deal of passion about Communism but not much useful information. He dashed off his second book, *The Whole of Their Lives*, in six weeks, hoping to cash in on the popularity of anti-Communism. The book was written in a lurid, potboiler style and contained none of the documentary evidence of *I Confess*. Whereas the autobiography depicted the Communist Party as composed of bumblers continually shooting themselves in the foot, the new book characterized it as "the Communist powerhouse" that would inevitably triumph over its soft-headed opponents.

Gitlow also moved from Manhattan, where he had run a letter shop, to the Mohegan Colony near Peekskill, New York, where his parents had maintained a home for forty years. That led to further tensions. The colony was composed largely of leftists who had moved up from New York City, and he and the other community members were barely able to maintain a semblance of peaceful coexistence. There was, however, one colony resident with whom Gitlow might have shared a special bond—Jay Lovestone, who lived less than half a mile away. Lovestone, though less conservative than Gitlow, had also become actively anti-Communist. But in spite of their unique shared history, they could not put aside their differences from the 1930s and never spoke to each other.

One of the ventures Gitlow undertook in the 1950s was a "Theater for Freedom," intended to counter what he saw as Communist domination of the cultural field. He got John Wayne to agree to be nominal chairman and issued announcements of its first show, "Raise the Red Curtain." But the theater had no funding and no real support from its supposed endorsers, and it never put on a production. In short, it was similar in form to the Communist fronts Gitlow had helped create in his Communist years—all letterhead, no cattle. In several ways, the Gitlow of the 1950s was similar to the Gitlow of the

1920s. His tone was urgent, imploring, often strident, and scornful of moderation. The language he used stayed largely the same, although the nouns were different.

It is tempting to describe Gitlow's life that way—an ideologue who changed ideologies. But that would be as one-sided as Gitlow himself tended to be. When he was in Moscow, Gitlow met Clara Zetkin, a famous German revolutionary and Comintern representative, and in *I Confess*, he recounts a message she sent to Stalin. Asked to explain her opposition to changes in the Comintern that Stalin had ordered, Zetkin replied, "I have always had the courage to take a stand even if I had to stand alone." Gitlow adopted that as his first principle, and it helps explains why, even after his turn toward intense anti-Communism, he referred often and with great pride to his two dramatic moments as a Communist: his trial speech and his rebuke to Stalin. Both times, he had been under great pressure to think about self-preservation and strike a conciliatory stance. Both times, he chose defiance. He had the courage to stand alone. That was the lesson he drew from these incidents in his Communist years, and he applied it even when making anti-Communist speeches to anti-Communist audiences.

Gitlow wrote an epitaph for himself, perhaps consciously, as part of a poem he submitted to the *National Review* three years before he died: "In its brief fiery ecstasy the fire-fly gives expression to the reason for its being. It strikes out courageously for the glory of the stars." A firefly striking out for the stars is a terrible metaphor for a poem but an apt one for Gitlow's life. From his youth, he always involved himself in the broadest, most far-reaching examinations of economic and political order. The passionate controversies surrounding American Communism that occupied most of his attention, though enormously important at the time, are already receding into history. But unintentionally, his life became intertwined with another issue of lasting significance—the expansion of the First Amendment. Although his conviction was upheld, the incorporation element, the centrality of the bad tendency doctrine, and the provocative nature of Holmes's dissent helped steer the Court toward greater protection for speech. The first line of Gitlow's obituary in the *New York Times*, which had supported his conviction, mentioned the case. The New York criminal anarchy law that was at the center of the legal argument was substantially revised on July 20, 1965 — one day after Gitlow died. His case was not the appointment with history he had imagined. But its legacy helped ensure that future Ben Gitlows would be able to express their views in whatever language and with whatever passion they saw fit, leaving the rest of us — as Clarence Darrow said at Gitlow's trial — to sort out the sense from the nonsense.

CHRONOLOGY

1891   Ben Gitlow born in New Jersey.

1892   Gitlow family moves to Bronx.

1901   President William McKinley assassinated in Buffalo.

1902   New York legislature passes Criminal Anarchy Act, in response to McKinley's assassination.

1904   Supreme Court in *U.S. ex rel. Turner v. Williams* upholds deportation of British anarchist John Turner.

1907   In *Patterson v. Colorado*, Oliver Wendell Holmes upholds contempt citation of newspaper editor critical of state courts, ruling that freedom of speech means freedom from prior restraint.

1909   Gitlow joins Socialist Party.

1915   In *Fox v. Washington*, Holmes writes opinion upholding conviction of John Fox for writing a pamphlet that, "by indirection," might have led to public nudity.

1917   Left-wing faction of Socialist Party meets in Brooklyn to consider forming a new party (January).

       Bolshevik revolution occurs in Russia (October).

       Gitlow, running as a Socialist, elected to represent Bronx in New York Assembly (November).

1918   Gitlow loses reelection bid.

1919   Holmes writes opinion upholding convictions of Socialist Party leaders Charles Schenck and Eugene Debs for antiwar, antidraft expression, holding that they created "clear and present danger" (March).

       New York legislature approves formation of Legislative Committee to Investigate Subversive Activities, known as the Lusk Committee (March).

       Left-wing Socialists meet to discuss forming Bolshevik-style party; Gitlow named to the group's National Council (June).

       Final version of "Left Wing Manifesto" published (July).

       Left wing splits from Socialist Party, forms two Communist parties. Gitlow helps create Communist Labor Party (September).

       Trials and convictions of anarchists Gust Alonen and Carl Paivio, charged with violating criminal anarchy law (October).

Supreme Court in *Abrams v. United States* votes to uphold conviction of New York anarchists for publishing leaflet opposing American intervention in Soviet Union; Holmes dissents, joined by Louis Brandeis (November).

Gitlow among hundreds arrested at New York rally celebrating anniversary of Bolshevik revolution; Gitlow charged with violating criminal anarchy law, along with Jim Larkin, Harry Winitsky, Isaac E. Ferguson, and Charles E. Ruthenberg (November).

1920   Trials and convictions of Gitlow (January), Winitsky (March), Larkin (April), and Ferguson and Ruthenberg (October).

1921   Appellate Division unanimously upholds Gitlow's conviction.

1922   Court of appeals upholds Gitlow's conviction; Benjamin Cardozo and Roscoe Pound dissent (July).

New York Court of Appeals orders new trial for Ferguson and Ruthenberg; none takes place, and they are freed (July).

1923   New York governor Al Smith pardons Larkin (January).

Gitlow v. New York argued in Supreme Court (April).

1924   Smith pardons Winitsky (January).

While free on bond, Gitlow marries Badana Zeitlin (December).

1925   Supreme Court issues decision upholding conviction in *Gitlow v. New York*; declares that First Amendment applies to states as well as federal government; Holmes writes dissent, which Brandeis joins (June).

Comintern names Ruthenberg head of Communist Party of United States (August).

Ben Gitlow pardoned and released from prison (December).

1927   Brandeis writes dissent in *Ruthenberg v. Michigan*, argued by anarchy codefendant Ferguson. Case mooted by Ruthenberg's death (March).

Jay Lovestone named acting party secretary following Ruthenberg's death (March).

Gitlow makes first trip to Moscow to attend Comintern meeting; meets with Bukharin (May).

Brandeis issues opinion in *Whitney v. California* using much of dissent intended for *Ruthenberg* (May).

1928   Gitlow returns to Moscow for meeting of Profintern (Red International of Labor Unions).

1929   Gitlow elected general secretary of Communist Party of United States (February).

Delegation, including Lovestone and Gitlow, arrives in Moscow to debate Comintern instructions to American Communist Party (April).

Stalin denounces Lovestone; demands that Americans support resolution calling themselves "Hooverites" and "Babbitts" (May).

Gitlow and Lovestone removed from leadership positions by Stalin (May).

Lovestone expelled from party (June).

Gitlow expelled from party (August).

1931   Supreme Court decides in *Stromberg v. California* that law against raising of red flag at youth camp is unconstitutional: "The maintenance of the opportunity for free political discussion . . . is a fundamental principle of our system."

1933   Gitlow splits with Lovestone, citing differences over Stalin.

1937   Supreme Court in *De Jonge v. Oregon* strikes down conviction of a Communist who led and spoke to a rally supporting a strike: "Peaceful assembly for lawful discussion cannot be made a crime" (January).

Supreme Court decides in *Herndon v. Lowry* that possession of Communist material alone is insufficient to demonstrate incitement: "The power of a state to abridge freedom of speech and assembly is the exception rather than the rule" (April).

1938   Show trial and execution of Bukharin lead Gitlow to disavow his Communist past.

1939   Gitlow testifies extensively before Dies Committee; publishes autobiography *I Confess.*

1951   In *Dennis v. United States*, Supreme Court upholds conviction of eleven Communist Party leaders, although Frankfurter writes that Holmes's *Gitlow* dissent "has been treated with the respect usually accorded to a decision." Gitlow writes to assistant attorney general supporting the verdict.

1957   In *Yates v. United States*, Supreme Court makes conviction of Communists more difficult.

1965   Ben Gitlow dies in Crompond, New York (July 19).

Criminal anarchy law under which Gitlow was convicted repealed by New York legislature (July 20).

1969   In *Brandenburg v. Ohio*, Supreme Court overturns *Whitney v. California* and, implicitly, *Gitlow v. New York*, holding that for speech to be criminal, it must incite to "imminent lawless action."

BIBLIOGRAPHICAL ESSAY

Note from the Series Editors: The following bibliographic essay contains the major primary and secondary sources the author consulted for this volume. We have asked all authors in the series to omit formal citations in order to make our volumes more readable, inexpensive, and appealing for students and general readers. In adopting this format, Landmark Law Cases and American Society follows the precedent of a number of highly regarded and widely consulted series.

The Supreme Court decision upholding the conviction of Benjamin Gitlow for violating New York's criminal anarchy law was the culmination of so many historical and legal events and the beginning of so many others that there are numerous bibliographic subcategories. Of course, an examination of the original trial, the appeals, and the Supreme Court decision is the starting point. The original trial, *People of the State of New York v. Benjamin Gitlow*, is on microfilm at the New York Supreme Court Law Library; librarian David Badertscher was extremely helpful in locating relevant material. Also on microfilm are the other criminal anarchy trials of those charged with Gitlow: *People v. Harry Winitsky*, *People v. James Larkin*, and *People v. Isaac E. Ferguson and Charles E. Ruthenberg*. For reasons explained in the text, the slightly earlier but highly relevant trial of anarchists Gust Alonen and Carl Paivio is also important in understanding the *Gitlow* case; that trial is also on microfilm at the New York Supreme Court Law Library. The two state-level appeals decisions—both upholding Gitlow's conviction—are, at the Appellate Division, *People of New York v. Benjamin Gitlow*, 195 A.D. 773; 187 N.Y.S. 783 (1921); and, at the court of appeals (where there were two dissenters), 234 N.Y. 132; 136 N.E. 317 (1922). The Supreme Court decision (268 U.S. 652, 4 S.Ct. 625 [1925]) is widely available online.

There are two Gitlow archives. Although both contain material covering his entire life, the archive at the Special Collections of the Murray Atkins Library at the University of North Carolina–Charlotte has more from his Communist period, ending roughly around 1936. The archive at the Hoover Institute has more on his post-Communist life. Both are invaluable. Of particular interest are the letters (at North Carolina–Charlotte) he wrote to his wife, Badana, while he was in Moscow during the showdown with Stalin and the successive drafts of *I Confess* (at the Hoover Institute), with the editing showing the evolution of his thinking during the months he spent writing. As a supplement to the archival material, Gitlow's September 1939 testimony before the Dies Committee is significant, especially when he provided documentary evidence. He testified again in July 1953, when the committee went by its better-known name of the House Un-American Activities Committee

(HUAC), but by that time, he was so distant from his Communist past that his testimony lacked the immediacy, and probably the accuracy, of his earlier statement. This point about the second HUAC testimony also applies to Gitlow's second book, *The Whole of Their Lives* (Boston: Western Islands Books, 1948). Written, as his son admitted, in an attempt to make money from the prominence of the domestic Communism issue, it is more lurid, based less on documents, and probably more creative with facts than his earlier book.

The most practical starting point in an examination of the *Gitlow* case may be the articles written by Harold Josephson. After her husband's death, Badana Gitlow donated his papers to Josephson, who wrote two extremely useful articles. "The Dynamic of Repression: New York during the Red Scare," 59 *Mid-America* 32 (1977), looks at all the criminal anarchy trials in New York; the second, "Political Justice during the Red Scare: The Trials of Benjamin Gitlow," in *American Political Trials*, ed. Michal Belknap (Westport, CT: Greenwood Press, 1981), is more exclusively focused on the *Gitlow* prosecution.

Of the many useful books summarizing the First Amendment debates of the period, the one that led me to consider writing a book on the *Gitlow* case was Richard Polenberg's *Fighting Faiths* (New York: Viking Penguin 1987). He follows the anarchists (and one Socialist) involved in *Abrams v. United States* before, during, and after their legal engagement and shows the reader what the case and its legacy meant to them. The writer who pioneered the study of pre–World War I speech-rights cases and is still their leading chronicler is David Rabban, first in his article "The Emergence of Modern First Amendment Doctrine," 50 *University of Chicago Law Review* 1207 (1983), and then in his book *Free Speech in Its Forgotten Years* (New York: Cambridge University Press, 1997). He also wrote "Free Speech in Progressive Social Thought," 74 *Texas Law Review* 951 (1996), describing how those who signed onto the war as a Progressive social venture wrestled with the speech-rights issue.

Many books describe the level of dissent during World War I and the large number of cases generated by it, including Margaret Blanchard, *Revolutionary Sparks* (New York: Oxford Press, 1992); Robert Justin Goldstein, *Political Repression in Modern America* (Urbana: University of Illinois Press, 2001); and Clement Werk, *Darkest before Dawn* (Albuquerque: University of New Mexico Press, 2005). Several other books trace the development of Supreme Court doctrine through these cases, focusing on the lower-level federal court judges who took a more expansive view of speech protection than did the Supreme Court majority and on the dissents of Oliver Wendell Holmes and Louis Brandeis. Among the most useful and recent are Mark Graber, *Transforming Free Speech: The Ambiguous Civil Libertarian Legacy* (Berkeley: University of California Press, 1991), although his negative view of Holmes seems one-sided, and Geoffrey Stone, *Perilous Times* (New York: W. W. Norton, 2004). Among the many articles discussing the Court's World War I speech-rights debate, the most significant for purposes of this project were Geoffrey Stone, "The Origins of the BAD Tendency Test: Free Speech in Wartime," 2002 *Supreme Court Review* 411 (1999), and Terry Heinrich, "*Gitlow* Redux: 'Bad Tendency' in the Great White North," 48 *Wayne Law Review* 1101 (2002), which has a lengthy and focused discussion of the *Gitlow* case. Other useful articles include Vincent Blasi, "The First Amendment and the Ideal of Civic Courage: The Brandeis Opinion in *Whitney v. California*," 29 *William and Mary Law Review* 653 (1983), and Bradley Bobertz, "The Brandeis Gambit: The Making of America's First Freedom (1909–1931)," 40 *William and Mary Law Review* 557 (1999), both on the connection between *Gitlow* and *Whitney*. See also David Bogen, "The Free Speech Metamorphosis of Mr. Justice Holmes," 11 *Hofstra Law Review* 97 (1982); David Cole, "Agon at Agora: Creative Misreadings in First Amendment Tradition," 95 *Yale Law Journal* 857 (1986); and G. Edward White, "Justice Holmes and the Modernization of Free Speech Jurisprudence: The Human Dimension," 80 *California Law Review* 391 (1992), all on Holmes's transformation from his earlier to later speech-rights decisions.

Several of these books and articles make a point of differentiating Holmes's views from those of Brandeis, with the standard argument being that, unlike Brandeis, Holmes voted to protect only ineffective speech. I make a brief counterargument in chapter 6 and list here thirteen post-*Abrams* cases with at least some First Amendment elements in which the two justices voted on the same side to overturn convictions:

Pierce v. United States, 252 U.S. 39 (1920)
Schaeffer v. United States, 362 U.S. 51 (1920)
U.S. ex rel. Milwaukee Social Democratic Publishing Co. v. Burleson, 256 U.S. 407 (1921) (separate dissents)
Leach v. Carlisle, 258 U.S. 138 (1922)
Gitlow v. New York (1925)
Ruthenberg v. Michigan (1927) (mooted)
Whitney v. California, 274 U.S. 357 (1927) (concurrence that was, in essence, a dissent)
Fisk v. Kansas, 274 U.S. 380 (1927) (voted with a unanimous Court)
Burns v. United States, 274 U.S. 328 (1927)
United States v. Schwimmer, 279 U.S. 644 (1929) (Sanford joined the dissent)
MacIntosh v. United States, 283 U.S. 605 (1931) (dissented with two others)
Stromberg v. California, 283 U.S. 359 (1931) (voted with the Court majority)
Near v. Minnesota, 283 U.S. 697 (1931) (voted with the Court majority)

The one case in which they differed was *Gilbert v. Minnesota*, 254 U.S. 325 (1920). Philippa Strum looks at Holmes's thinking and what might have caused the disagreement between the two in *Beyond Progressivism* (Lawrence: University Press of Kansas, 1993) and "Brandeis: The Public Activist and Freedom of Speech," *Brandeis Law Journal* 45 (2006–2007). I attribute the difference between Holmes and Brandeis in *Gilbert* to Holmes's long struggle against Fourteenth Amendment judicial activism. Holmes's formulation of judicial restraint is well described in Paul Kens, *Judicial Power and Reform Politics: The Anatomy of* Lochner v. New York (Lawrence: University Press of Kansas, 1990). Holmes's private thoughts on *Gitlow* are expressed in his letters to Harold Laski and Frederick Pollock, in *Holmes-Laski Letters* (1953) and *Holmes-Pollock Letters* (1961), both edited by Mark DeWolfe Howe (Cambridge, MA: Harvard University Press). Examining the Oliver Wendell Holmes Papers at Harvard and the Louis Brandeis Papers at Harvard and at the University of Louisville helps explain the thinking of both men in their First Amendment cases.

One criticism of Holmes's *Gitlow* dissent is that he did not interact seriously with Edward Sanford's opinion. The best examples of that position are in Harry Kalven, *A Worthy Tradition: Free Speech in America* (New York: Harper and Row, 1988), and Gary Craig Turley's dissertation "Free Speech and the Doctrine of Incorporation: The Role of *Gitlow v. New York* in Modern First Amendment Theory" (University of Oregon, 1989). Another approach critical of Holmes is Alexander Tsesis, *Destructive Messages: How Hate Speech Paves the Way for Harmful Social Movements* (New York: New York University Press, 2002). Tsesis argues that the *Gitlow* dissent should be read in light of Holmes's forays into social Darwinism. For a useful response, see Anuj Desai, "Attacking *Brandenburg* with History: Does the Long-Term Harm of Biased Speech Justify a Criminal Statute Suppressing It?" 55 *Federal Communication Law Journal* 2 (2003), who discusses the reevaluation of Holmes and *Gitlow* by proponents of speech codes.

The *Gitlow* case is best known for its "incorporation" assertion by the Court. Raoul Berger, *The 14th Amendment and the Bill of Rights* (Norman: University of Oklahoma Press, 1989), and Michael Kent Curtis, *No State Shall Abridge* (Durham, NC: Duke University Press, 1986), discuss the intentions of the framers of the Fourteenth Amendment. Richard Cortner, *The Supreme Court and the Second Bill of Rights* (Madison: University of Wisconsin Press, 1981), discusses that issue plus the long process by which the Supreme Court nationalized most of the Bill of Rights. Charles Warren, "The New 'Liberty' under the Fourteenth Amendment," *Harvard Law Review* 39, 5 (1926), may have been the first to recognize the far-ranging ramifications of the incorporation assertion in *Gitlow*. Klaus Heberle in "From Gitlow to Near: Judicial 'Amendment' by Absent-minded Incrementalism," *Journal of Politics* 34 (1972), focuses on the movement from stipulation in *Gitlow* to accepted precedent with little argument or notice. Lewis Laska, "Mr. Justice Sanford and the

Fourteenth Amendment," *Tennessee Historical Quarterly* 33 (1974), goes over what little there is to say about Sanford's thinking in making the *Gitlow* stipulation.

Cortner also provides useful details on the major speech-rights cases following *Gitlow*: *Whitney, Stromberg, De Jonge,* and *Herndon*. For more on the *Whitney* case, including biographical material, see Woodrow Whitten, "Trial of Anita Whitney," *Pacific Historical Review* 15 (1946), and Lisa Reubens, "The Patrician Radical: Charlotte Anita Whitney," *California History* 65 (1986). For the *Herndon* case, see Charles Martin, *The Angelo Herndon Case and Southern Justice* (Baton Rouge: Louisiana State University Press, 1976). My information about the later life of Yetta Stromberg came from personal communication with her relative, Judith Bronfman, who is completing a documentary movie about Stromberg entitled *Land of Orange Groves and Jails*. Ronald Collins and David Skover provide the most in-depth coverage of the *Ruthenberg* case in "*Ruthenberg v. Michigan*: An Introduction," in *The Louis Brandeis Papers:* Ruthenberg v. Michigan (Harvard Law School On-line Library, 2010). The *De Jonge* case is a book waiting to be written.

The events and arguments in the criminal anarchy trials will be opaque without an understanding of the historical backdrop. The best place to begin is Gitlow's autobiography *I Confess* (New York: E. P. Dutton, 1939). The book concentrates on his life, beginning as a pioneering American Communist to his 1929 confrontation with Stalin and subsequent expulsion from the party. Written very soon after Gitlow first broke with Communism, the book's standpoint is sometimes confusing—he reserves special venom for his opponents within the party, even though he has rejected the premises he once espoused in the factional conflicts that dominate the book. But *I Confess* is very clear about the enthusiasm for the Russian Revolution that led some leftists in this country to try to reshape American Socialism in the Bolshevik mold. It gives his perspectives on the decisions at his trial, and it ends with a thrilling reconstruction of the 1929 meeting in Moscow after which he, Jay Lovestone, and other leading party figures were expelled. Another participant expelled after that meeting was Bertram Wolfe, who recounts the events in *A Life in Two Centuries* (New York: Stein and Day, 1981). Written forty years after Gitlow's account and after Wolfe, like Gitlow, had become conservative and fiercely anti-Communist, the book looks back on the events with some humor and detachment. It should be noted that both books contain quotations that are not taken from documents; they are the authors' best reconstructions many years later and should not be understood as literal.

On the Red Scare era that produced both the criminal anarchy trials discussed here and the Palmer raids, two older books are still good starting points: Lawrence Chamberlain, *Loyalty and Legislative Action* (Ithaca, NY: Cornell University Press, 1937), and Eldridge Dowell, *A History of Criminal*

Syndicalism Legislation in the United States (Baltimore: Johns Hopkins University Press, 1939). More recent works are Julian Jaffe, *Crusade against Radicalism* (New York: Kennikat Press, 1972), and Todd Pfannestiehl, *Rethinking the Red Scare* (New York: Routledge Press, 2003). A good recent popularization that covers the *Gitlow* trial in the context of the Palmer raids is Kenneth Ackerman, *Young J. Edgar* (New York: Carroll and Graf, 2007). It is also worth looking at *The Report of the Joint Legislative Committee Investigating Seditious Activities*, 4 vols. (New York: J. B. Lyon, 1920) — better known as the Lusk Committee report — even though it is almost comically padded with extraneous material. Archibald Stevenson's explanation of the legal theory of the criminal anarchy prosecutions, "The World War and Freedom of Speech," *New York Times Literary Supplement*, February 18, 1925, is also interesting reading.

The starting point for studying American Communism in the 1920s is Theodore Draper's two volumes: *The Roots of American Communism* (New York: Viking Press, 1957) and *American Communism and Soviet Russia* (New York: Viking Press, 1960). That is not to say that there is consensus about his conclusions; for a discussion of the ongoing controversy about Draper, read "The Elephant in the Living Room: Theodore Draper and the Historiography of American Communism," *American Communist History* 8 (2005). It summarizes several decades of the controversy, albeit from a pro-Draper perspective (which I share). A useful repository containing a huge number of original documents from this period is available at www.marxisthistory.org, organized by Tim Davenport.

Other useful works on early American Communism include James Weinstein, *The Decline of Socialism in America* (New York: Monthly Review Press, 1967); Irving Howe and Lewis Coser, *The American Communist Party: A Critical Analysis* (New York: Da Capo, 1974); Ted Morgan, *Reds: McCarthyism in Twentieth Century America* (New York: Random House, 2003); and Bryan Palmer, *James P. Cannon and the Origins of the American Revolutionary Left, 1890–1928* (Urbana: University of Illinois Press, 2007). For more information on the 1929 confrontation with Stalin in Moscow and its aftermath, see Robert Alexander, *The Right Opposition: The Lovestonites and the International Communist Opposition of the 1930s* (Westport, CT: Greenwood Press, 1981), and Ted Morgan's biography of Jay Lovestone, *A Covert Life: Jay Lovestone: Communist, Anti-Communist, and Spymaster* (New York: Random House, 1999).

Biographical information on some of the other principals in the criminal anarchy trials includes several books on Jim Larkin: Emmet Larkin (no relation), *James Larkin: Irish Labor Leader* (Cambridge, MA: MIT Press, 1965) and Emmet O'Conner, *James Larkin* (Cork, Ireland: Cork University Press, 2003). There is also a very entertaining chapter on Larkin in Bertram Wolfe, *Strange Communists I Have Known* (London: Allen and Unwin Press, 1966). Wolfe is able to write sympathetically about his former leftist friends long after he himself became passionately anti-Communist. There is no biography of Charles E. Ruthenberg, although there is extensive coverage of him in Draper's books. Even more disappointing, virtually nothing has been written about Isaac E. Ferguson, Ruthenberg's codefendant in New York and his lawyer in that trial and in the Supreme Court case.

Besides Hoover and North Carolina, other archives contain some relevant papers. The most important is the Tamiment Center at New York University, which has files on Harry Winitsky, Charles Recht, and Abraham Shiplacoff, as well as microfilm copies of records of the Communist Party of the United States that had been stored in Moscow, out of public sight, for decades. The Lilly Library at Indiana University contains the Max Eastman Papers; Eastman wrote the foreword to *I Confess* and exchanged several letters with Gitlow. The Immigrant History Research Center at the University of Minnesota has information about Carl Paivio but not, unfortunately, about Gust Alonen. The Rare Books Collection at Emory University has the papers and notes that Draper used to write his history, which include additional sources about the 1929 Moscow meeting.

The most engaging description of the conditions of Jewish immigrants on the Lower East Side of Manhattan is David Von Drehle, *Triangle: The Fire that Changed America* (New York: Atlantic Monthly Press, 2003). Good discussions of the left-wing Jewish political culture that emerged from that experience are in Melech Epstein (a Gitlow contemporary), *The Jews and Communism* (New York: H. Wolfe, 1959), and Arthur Liebman, *Jews and the Left* (New York: John Wiley and Son, 1979).

Finally, I interviewed or communicated with a number of people who provided useful information. Most important was the extended interview with Benjamin Gitlow Jr., whose reflections were invaluable. Other members of the Gitlow family who communicated with me included Lawrence Fruchter, Gitlow's nephew, and Stuart Gitlow, a more distant relative who provided a family tree. Bill Schilling at the New York Board of Elections provided the vote totals for Gitlow's win in the 1917 assembly election, his losing reelection bid in 1918, and the victory of another Socialist in 1919. I communicated in person or by e-mail with Robert Alexander, Tim Davenport, Judith Branfman, Eleanor Jackson Piehl (lawyer in the *Epton v. New York* criminal anarchy case, before the law was repealed), and Herbert Rommerstein and Emmett Larkin (both of whom met Gitlow).

INDEX

Gilbert v. Minnesota; Schenck v. United States; Sedition Act Amendments of 1918
World War II, 134–135, 148

Yale Law Review, 124

Yates v. United States, 139, 155

Zeitlin, Badana, 8, 122, 145, 146, 147, 154
Zetkin, Clara, 150
Zinman, Joseph, 57